Sober Letters To My Drunken Self

Ed Latimore

Copyright © 2018 by Edward Latimore

All rights reserved. This book or any portion thereof may not be reproduced or used in any manner whatsoever without the express written permission of the publisher except for the use of brief quotations in a book review.

Set in Futura and PMN Caecilia

Printed in the United States of America

First Printing, 2018

Ed Latimore
www.edlatimore.com

This book details the author's personal experiences with and opinions about alcohol and alcoholism.

The author is not a healthcare provider.

The author and publisher are providing this book and its contents on an "as is" basis and make no representations or warranties of any kind with respect to this book or its contents. The author and publisher disclaim all such representations and warranties, including for example warranties of merchantability and healthcare for a particular purpose. In addition, the author and publisher do not represent or warrant that the information accessible via this book is accurate, complete or current.

The statements made about products and services have not been evaluated by the U.S. Food and Drug Administration. They are not intended to diagnose, treat, cure, or prevent any condition or disease. Please consult with your own physician or healthcare specialist regarding the suggestions and recommendations made in this book.

Except as specifically stated in this book, neither the author or publisher, nor any authors, contributors, or other representatives will be liable for damages arising out of or in connection with the use of this book. This is a comprehensive limitation of liability that applies to all damages of any kind, including (without limitation) compensatory; direct, indirect or consequential damages; loss of data, income or profit; loss of or damage to property and claims of third parties.

You understand that this book is not intended as a substitute for consultation with a licensed healthcare practitioner, such as your physician. Before you begin any healthcare program, or change your lifestyle in any way, you will consult your physician or another licensed healthcare practitioner to ensure that you are in good health and that the examples contained in this book will not harm you.

This book provides content related to physical and/or mental health issues. As such, use of this book implies your acceptance of this disclaimer.

Edward Latimore

This book is for everyone who never gave up on me—especially when you should have.

This book is for everyone thinking of giving up on themselves—especially when they should not.

Table of Contents

10   **WHAT THIS BOOK IS AND HOW TO USE IT**
Quick words before you read further into this book to help you get the most out of it.

13   **THE GREAT CHALLENGES**
While your environment poses a formidable threat, you don't stand a chance if you don't realize that you are the greatest challenge you'll face on your road to recovery.

19   **YOU CAN GET DRUNK BUT YOU CAN'T HIDE**
Every drinker thinks they can drink away their insecurities and social anxiety. This is why it's alcohol is often called *"liquid courage"*. But you can't drown your anxiety in alcohol and you can't hide from your fears in a bottle.

25   **WHY DO YOU DRINK?**
All alcoholics have an unhealthy relationship with alcohol, but why did we start drinking like this? Each of these reasons is a stand-alone motivation for heavy drinking, but it's also possible that each can be represented to varying degrees within the individual.

29   **VICES TO VIRTUE**
The same thing that drives your alcoholic destruction can drive sober accomplishments. The energy of a bad lifestyle can be redirected and rechanneled toward developing stellar habits. Obsession is neither good or bad. Only the subject makes it so.

33   **THE NEVER ENDING GUILT**
No one warns you about the guilt that your sobriety brings with it. Without the fog of alcohol clouding your conscience, you can clearly consider the destructiveness of your intoxicated behavior. This pains you, but there is a solution.

39   **REGRETS AND WHAT YOU THINK YOU'RE MISSING**
Even though I knew that I needed to stop drinking, I stalled on making the decision because I feared missing out on the things I thought were important to my life. However, in the long-term, these things are not only meaningless, but they are keeping you from reaching your full potential.

45   **ONE DAY AT A TIME**
When you stop drinking, things don't suddenly improve. You've merely put yourself on the right track. Only by taking things one day at a time will make actual progress and a real difference in your life.

51 **MONSTERS BENEATH THE SURFACE**
Everyone thinks horrible things, yet our conscious mind keeps sentry over our dark urges. Alcohol erodes this gatekeeper to our subconscious and makes everyone's life a living hell. Alcoholics, in particular, know these monsters beneath the surface all too well.

55 **I KNOW WHO I AM. WHO ARE YOU?**
You've been an alcoholic so long that you don't know who you are. A large part of getting sober is believing that you have the ability to be someone different than who you are now. You will make the change. I know this because I made the change and we are the same person battling this monster of addiction.

61 **THE THREE THINGS YOU NEED TO STOP DRINKING**
This is the closest thing to a surefire solution to alcoholism I've found. In truth, it's how any meaningful change is made. If you do these three things, your chances of sobriety skyrocket.

69 **DRUNK THOUGHTS, SOBER DECISIONS**
The problems you cause while under the influence are problematic, but an even greater issue is the mindset that you will have as long as getting drunk is an option. You'll do things while apparently sober that only a drunk mind could conceive off. Understanding this is key to understanding yourself and why alcohol has a grip on you.

73 **AN ALCOHOL PROBLEM OR PROBLEMS ON ALCOHOL**
Some of us can't put the bottle down, while some of us only have issues when we pick it up. This is a subtle difference but a significant one. Understanding the difference will help you understand yourself. Regardless of which problem you have, the solutions are remarkably similar.

79 **A PRODUCT OF YOUR ENVIRONMENT**
Personalities, habits, and tendencies are not formed in a vacuum. Who you are, how you respond, and what you think is all influenced by your environment. While your personality is innate and mostly genetic, the expression of it depends on what you've been exposed to. Understanding this feedback mechanism is crucial for dealing with your drinking.

85 **HOW TO HAVE FUN AND SOCIALIZE SOBER**
In modern civilization, people build their entire social lives around drinking. It's no surprise that most people don't know how to socialize alcohol-free and have fun sober. The most important thing for you to realize about your inability to socialize without alcohol is that it's all in your head.

91 **CONNECTION WITH THE REAL YOU**
You are a person who, at one point, lived a life of sobriety. Even if was only when you were a young adult. Even as an alcoholic, you've experienced moments of a life that does not bind you to constant consumption. A key to sobriety is getting in touch with this part of you and nurturing its development.

What This Book Is And How To Use It

I wrote this book as if I was able to go back in time and talk to myself when I started to suspect I had an alcohol problem. As a result, some of the letters are written in the first person. However, this book is also a guide for others. To achieve this goal, other essays are written in the third person as necessary. This allows me to give you the advice and guidance I desperately wish someone had given me when I was showing the signs of alcoholism.

While I think every essay contains valuable wisdom and advice, it's not necessary to read this book from cover to cover. Where you start will depend on where you are in your journey. Some people have given sobriety a serious thought, but need a push over the edge. Some people are in their first week on the wagon and aren't sure they're going to make it. Some of you have been dry for a while but still have trouble coping with the lifestyle adjustment. It doesn't matter. All that is required to get something from this book is a desire to stop drinking.

What if you're a raging alcoholic? This is the type of person that feels like they wouldn't survive without at least one alcoholic drink per day. I believe this book can help you. Perhaps you'll need more than the words in these pages, but just reading them proves that you want to stop. Sometimes all you need is the intent to change and the commitment to see it through.

There is one other person who might read this book; the stone-cold skeptic. This is the person that thinks that booze is a harmless part of life and can't understand why anyone would ever want to stop drinking. They bought this book to give it a one-star review without even reading it.

That's ok though. As anyone who deviates from the norm knows—the norm in this case being drinking—that people will react strongly to things that are different. Some of these people, who have no interest in sobriety, may give it a second thought once they read through the book.

What This Book Isn't

It's very important to state what this book is not. This book is a not a persuasive text. I have no interest in convincing someone to give up drinking. If a person is not ready to stop drinking, they won't make the effort to abstain from alcohol based on a few stories from a recovering alcoholic.

It is not my goal to coax or cajole someone into sobriety. There are several organizations today who make this their primary mission, but it's not mine. My intention is not to make you go somewhere you aren't interested in going. If you want to get to the sobriety, then I am more than happy to teach you how to get there.

This book is not intended to replace professional medical advice, diagnosis, or treatment. If you have a drinking-related health issue, don't take my advice if it's going to alter your course of medically prescribed treatment. While I can't imagine anything in this book will clash with any medical advice, the law says I must state this point clearly: I am not a medical or health professional—just a guy with some ideas and techniques (albeit very powerful and effective) about how to control drinking.

You won't find any moral, ethical, or spiritual arguments here. Appealing to a personal philosophy feels too much like persuasion for me. I judge the effectiveness of a method based on the number of people it can be unequivocally effective for. If it requires conversion to new religion, then it's not useful for a person who wants to stop drinking without changing other parts of their life.

Along those lines, this is not a therapeutic text. The book isn't going to ask you to do any soul-searching into the deeper reasons of why you drink. I have no issue with therapy for resolving interpersonal issues, but I am not a therapist. Therefore, I cannot administer therapy. Even if I could, I wouldn't do it via book.

My approach to a problem is very simple: I see what has worked, I try it myself with modifications and improvements where I see fit, and then I teach others what I have learned if they have the same problem. There is no room for discussing how I feel along the way.

Lastly, this is not a book for the immature. I will directly deliver my advice and methods. I draw only from my experience to give you something that can be of great value to your life. Though it is meant to be as simple as possible, few things worth doing are so easy that everyone can do them. If they were, then they wouldn't be worthwhile. There is advice in this book that will make you uncomfortable and stressed, but it will help you if sobriety is what you truly desire.

This requires the maturity to recognize that you picked up this book believing that I offer you something of value. You picked up this book with the belief that I know what I'm talking about. Trust in the process. Most importantly, take it one day at a time.

The Great Challenges

A great challenge you'll encounter in your sobriety is yourself. Even if you have the most toxic environment and enabling peers imaginable, the most challenging part of getting sober will be maintaining your desire to stay sober. It's easy to swear off drinking when you're nursing a hangover, looking through drunk texts, or repairing your reputation in the morning. It's a lot more difficult after things have been going well and you think you can handle it.

A great challenge you'll face is having the courage to say you no longer want to drink. Even if you silently declare it to yourself, making the declaration is an important and powerful first step. It takes more courage than you can imagine to look yourself in the mirror and admit that you have a problematic relationship with alcohol.

Society has told you that there's nothing wrong with excess drinking. It continues to ignore the role that alcohol plays in physical and sexual assault. You're made to feel like an outcast because you question such a self-destructive ritual. It's alright to feel like resisting this onslaught is an impossible task.

This just means that you're being realistic. This realism is what originally lead you to make the decision to get sober. You saw the end result of continued heavy drinking and decided that you don't want to be there. It's natural to think it's going to be easy to abstain from alcohol, but when things are going well you will forget how bad they can become.

You'll forget the hangovers. You'll forget the guilt. You'll forget the disorientation and powerlessness that alcohol causes. When you forget these things, then it's easy to believe that you can handle another drink.

After I realized I had a drinking problem, it took me a while to get sober. There were many reasons why, but a significant factor was that I always forgot how bad things would get for me. I'd stop drinking and things would get better. At this point, I figured that as long as I only had a few drinks, then I'd be alright.

The problem is that it's never *"only a few drinks"*. My lack of moderation is one of the main reasons I needed to quit. But this realization is useless if you don't do something about it. I believe that quitting alcohol is the easy part. Adhering to that commitment until it becomes a habit is the hard part.

You may have the best of intentions, but your environment is one of the greatest challenges you'll face. Changing your environment is difficult if you're extroverted. Even if you aren't an extrovert who needs to be part of a social scene to feel alive, many of us drink to avoid loneliness and isolation. This is especially problematic for younger people who want to stop drinking.

A great challenge you'll face is the new life you must lead. What isn't immediately obvious to the alcoholic is how much of their daily decisions revolve around alcohol. You stay in because you're exhausted from drinking the night before. You organize social events and work functions around alcohol. Even many of the people in your life at the moment are there because you met them while inebriated. As a result, maintenance of these relationships mandates that your socialization must always be infused with alcohol.

I believe this is why I kept many friends I had before I started drinking, but I have almost none of the ones I made during my heaviest drinking years. Our commonality was drinking. Once that was eliminated, I became a person different from the alcoholic they originally met. Furthermore, there was nothing left to hold our friendship together now that alcohol was no longer part of my life.

When we look at other parts of our lives, this appears obvious. We make friends in high school that we never talk to again. The only commonality we had was high school. Once that's gone, the relationship quickly follows suit. This relationship is no different from alcohol. What's surprising for many people is how different things are in non-drinking related parts of your life.

A great challenge you'll face is your new clarity and focus. When you aren't constantly drinking, you'll have more energy. You'll be able to pour yourself into lingering projects and goals. It's a unique combination of two distinct problems: you have more energy, but no interest in the common activities of an alcoholic—the things that you used to do. You must find new ways to invest this surplus energy.

When I got sober, I was fortunate. I just started working on my physics degree, was training for professional boxing, doing weekend drills for the Army National Guard, an engineering internship, writing for my website, and developing a romantic relationship. Looking back on my first year of sobriety, I realize that a reason I could perform at this level is that I simply had more energy. I was so committed to my sobriety and improving my life that I never gave myself a chance to relapse. I lived and breathed anything that kept me away from my old life and habits.

While I don't recommend that you take on this hellish level of work, you do need to find something. A friend of mine once said to me *"an addict by himself is in bad company"*. The worst thing you can do once you get sober is become a hermit. The new energy you have must be directed towards improving your life—especially the areas that sustained the most damage from your alcoholic lifestyle.

The great challenge you'll face is building this new life. You'll either need to engage in new hobbies or reconnect yourself with old ones. You are effectively reinventing yourself. As part of this reinvention, you'll also have to reinvent how you spend your free time. Finding hobbies is easy, but you have to do more than that. Getting a new hobby is just one part. Finding new people and doing said hobby with them is another matter entirely.

Most adults stopped exercising the *"make a new friend"* muscle right after college. You're probably like most adults. Not only will you have to make new friends, but you have to do it without the social aegis of alcohol. What never ceases to amaze me is how often people ask, *"How am I supposed to make friends if I don't drink?"*

If you ever find yourself wondering how you'll socialize without alcohol, you're not alone. It's not impossible. It's just different because you haven't done it in a long time—and you have to do it. Otherwise, you'll spend your sober time alone or you won't be sober for very long. Neither of these choices are appealing. This brings me to the next challenge you'll face.

One of your greatest challenges will be getting to know yourself all over again. At the most fundamental level, you have no idea what you like and dislike. You don't know who you like or dislike. All you know is that alcohol makes any activity bearable and any person tolerable. Think about all of the shitty people and places you've put up with for the possibility of alcohol.

The strange thing about this is that the alcohol doesn't even have to be free. Think about all the time you've spent on the bar stool, surrounded by other people drinking the evening away. Some of these people will become your *"friend"*, but without the unifying force of alcohol, you have almost nothing in common with these strangers.

This is also going to affect the people you find yourself romantically entangled with. As an alcoholic, you don't actually like most of them but they do provide sex and like to drink. This works well, but as you grow, you're going realize something about yourself—you're a surprisingly low key person.

There's a lot about yourself that you don't know. The longer you've been drinking, the more you've morphed your personality to adapt to what's available to you as a result of your choices and lifestyle. You may find, as I did, your romantic interests aren't quite what you believed they were. You were merely settling for what's available in the pool you had to select from.

Ultimately, the greatest challenge is the person in the mirror. The alcoholic version of you is the version of yourself that you're most familiar with. It's your comfort zone. The first steps of sobriety are miserable, not because of any physical withdraw, but because of psychological discomfort.

The desire is to relieve that discomfort the quickest way you know how . This has always been through alcohol. When you move from the known to the unknown, by definition, the journey is filled with uncertainty. The gap of uncertainty—the transformation of the old you to the new—is the hardest part. This is where you've left old habits behind but new ones have yet to define you. This is when you're in the most danger of relapsing.

Sobriety, in this regard, builds momentum. It grows like an exponential function. Yes, you take things one day at a time, but each day gets a little easier than the last—even if only by an infinitesimally small amount. Each day you grow a little more sure of yourself, the decision you made, and the new life you've chosen.

Until that point, there are questions. In truth, the questions never go away. What happens is you become more confident that you answered them correctly. You know this because each day the quality of your life improves. The problem is that change is painful, so in your early days of sobriety, the experience of change makes you wonder if you've made the right decision.

A greater challenge you face is convincing the person in the mirror that it's all worth it. I wondered this for a long time. Was it REALLY worth giving up the inclusion of alcohol in my life? While I wondered, I continued drinking. Each time I drank, I reminded myself of how low the quality of my life was as a result of behavior while under the influence of alcohol.

When I was sober, I never had any problems. I never got into trouble, embarrassed myself or woke up with regret while sober. These things only happened when I drank. I figured it was only a matter of time before I lost my closest friends. I could deal with everything else, but this was a toll I was unwilling to pay. Preserving these relationships is ultimately what pushed me over the edge into sobriety.

Sobriety is a lifestyle. While different lifestyles can co-exist, your challenge will be introducing the new you to your old surroundings. Some succeed, most fail, but all try. You will be no different.

You can get pretty low, but there's no reason to hit rock bottom. You can skate on thin ice, but you don't have to fall through to realize that how you're living will ruin you. Degrade my character and social standing. More importantly, understanding this desire allows me to help others with a similar struggle.

You Can Get Drunk But You Can't Hide

This specific note is not here to place blame. Placing blame is a weak and useless reaction to a problem. It causes you to forfeit the ability to learn from your mistakes. Making mistakes is a part of being human; learning from them is a privilege. I wrote this letter to help you learn from your life and other matters outside of your control which prompted your heavy drinking.

While there's nothing you can currently do with this information, you can, however, use this information to help others who may be struggling. Even though every addict has a different story, there are certain commonalities; one that is critical is the desire for acceptance.

Drinking to Fit In, Or Fitting In to Drink

The desire for acceptance is analogous to the *"chicken/egg"* problem: Do people with the desire to fit in behave recklessly to gain acceptance OR do people behave recklessly and therefore earn the acceptance of others with similar living standards? Normally, I don't think about this problem because I don't see its usefulness in attaining sobriety. Generally, evaluating WHY you're drinking comes AFTER you've realized your unhealthy relationship with alcohol.

Once you recognize this unhealthy relationship, you will start to see its manifestation in other people. This grants you tremendous power in helping others get sober. You may be one of the only people who can prevent someone from becoming a drunk and ruining their lives.

I eventually took some time to consider what prompted my drinking. This includes not just the part of my life that I spent drinking to excess, but also the parts where I consumed moderate and socially acceptable amounts of alcohol. My first drinks were not motivated out of curiosity; I drank because I thought it would make me cool. I suspect that many people consume alcohol for similar reasons. They drink or do drugs to belong, not because they want to alter their state of mind.

This is a natural human desire, for we are social animals. This desire becomes problematic when it serves as a means rather than an end. You're going to have many problems in your life if you do things just to fit in, rather than finding a group which naturally aligns with your choices. Nowhere is this more apparent than with alcohol consumption.

Rather than pursuing activities which you naturally enjoy (and becoming someone who lives based upon values which naturally resonate with you), you fail to discover an identity based on what's important to you. All your likes, dislikes, interests, and hobbies are ruled by what will allow you to fit in with the group, whose approval you crave.

In my situation, I craved the acceptance of 20-something-year-olds who represented my first chance to really feel like I belonged. This need for acceptance is yet another example of the saying *"the thing which drove you to drink can also drive you to greatness"*.

I've always wanted to fit in and be considered a *"cool kid"*. When this drive was harnessed positively, I pushed myself to the edges of my physical, mental, and emotional development. If the virtues of my innate personality weren't enough for me to fit in, I would try to earn approval with my achievements.

When my urge to be accepted took the path of least resistance, I stumbled down a path of alcoholism and self-destructive behavior. Always trying to be the one who drank more than everyone else is what happened when I could find no other outlet for acceptance. When people would cheer on my heavy drinking, or invite me to parties so that I could live up to my reputation as a hardcore partier, this satisfied my urge for recognition. More importantly, it satisfied my desire for approval and acceptance.

At the end of the day, being alone is my worst fear. I don't know if this fear ever will leave me. A longtime friend of mine perfectly summed up this feeling:

"Better to drink with assholes than to drink alone."

I knew what I needed in order to progress during this period of my life. However, I was too afraid of missing out. Sometimes, I think back to all the gym sessions and morning runs which I struggled to get out of bed for. I knew the requirements to be a better fighter, but I still didn't want to miss out on socializing and drinking which made me feel like I belonged.

It's easy to see why I felt like I needed to fit in. I spent much of my childhood as an outcast bullied, and mocked. These events contributed to my desire to fit in as an adult. A lack of relationship with my family led to my search for a group I felt I could belong to. I became addicted to acceptance and I saw alcohol as a way to connect with people in a way that I'd never been able to before.

Understanding why I feel this way does not allow me to reverse time and change my past. However, it does give me an advantage in dealing with my alcoholism. Understanding my need for acceptance allows me to focus on more positive ways to attain it. I'll never be able to shed the desire for acceptance, but I can pursue it in ways that elevate rather.

The failure to differentiate between various addictions happens to many alcoholics; at the very least, I know this happened to me. At some point, I was unable to separate my longing for acceptance from my longing for alcohol. It's no coincidence that I was in a long-term relationship the last time I stopped drinking for any length of time. I am now sober and also in a long-term relationship. Perhaps I've attained the sense of acceptance and belonging which I originally sought through drinking.

Proof of this can be found when I lived alone in Los Angeles. My heaviest drinking occurred when I lived there, alone, and without a driver's license. L.A. is not a city for a person to live in without a driver's license, especially without any friends. Maybe I could have gone out more often, but instead, I remained under the influence for a large part of most days. During this time, I regularly went through a box of wine and a few *"forties"* every two days or so. Why did I drink like this?

I drank like this because it reminded me of when I was accepted and did not feel lonely. I associated the feeling of belonging with the consumption of alcohol to the point where I could not distinguish them. On an intellectual level, I knew that drinking did not bring me closer to any other human being. Emotionally, I was operating on habits that were agitated by an intense desire to alleviate my discomfort.

This also worked in reverse. During most of the time I spent drinking, I didn't know how to experience strong emotions independently of alcohol. This happened whether the emotional stimulus was positive or negative. To me, someone's death was the same as winning a fight. Whether mourning a loss or celebrating a victory, emotional expression didn't feel complete without booze. Why this happens is not as obvious as the reverse situation. However, this is where the most well-known components of addiction manifest themselves.

People drink after a hard day. They also drink to celebrate. This ritual inadvertently breeds addiction. You have now hijacked your *"emotional tolerance."* Emotional tolerance is a term, which I created to explain exactly what happened to me. It also embodies what I believe happens to many others who have a poor relationship with alcohol.

When you use alcohol to augment or extinguish your emotional state, you rob yourself of the ability to independently manage your emotional state. If you engage in this behavior for long enough, you completely lose your ability to manage your emotions. Happiness doesn't feel as uplifting and sadness doesn't feel as cathartic. This is an ominous sign that you have developed a tolerance for alcohol which inevitably leads to dependency.

The tolerance is not only limited to your intoxicated emotional experiences, but it includes your sober experiences as well. Your emotions are miscalibrated to your reality. I refer to this as *"having the sunglasses on"*. The effect of alcohol on your emotional state is not unlike the effect that sunglasses have on light.

You can see through your sunglasses, but the light is dim. You are limited from experiencing the full color and vibrancy of the world. If you wear the sunglasses for long enough, you forget the colors of basic scenery like the green grass or the blue sky.

As a result of this transformation, you might even argue that the sky is pink and the grass is black. Wearing the sunglasses for so long has halted your ability to tell right from wrong. Ultimately, alcohol prevents people from correctly assessing and dealing with their emotional states.

If I felt socially awkward somewhere, I drank to feel more comfortable. Similarly, if I hit on a girl and faced rejection, I consumed alcohol. That was simply how I dealt with negative emotions. However, the effect did not end there.

For a while, I had no idea how to celebrate good events in my life without alcohol. I got a raise at work? Time to drink! It's my birthday? Let's drink! I just won a fight!? I have to drink!!! Alcohol prevented me from truly feeling and experiencing the most joyous things in my life. Since alcohol is no longer an option, I am forced to deal with all of my emotions. Similarly, when you take off your sunglasses, there is a degree of pain, but the world is way more enjoyable.

Ultimately, the desire to fit in and not be alone drove a lot of my drinking. At the time, I was not capable of analyzing this; however, I still suspected it, especially as my situation worsened. An interesting (yet not entirely unexpected) experience occurred when I accepted the primary factor which drove my alcoholism: I tried to hide in even more alcohol.

I'll never forget how I started spending Christmas: for a few years, my ritual involved finding an open bar on Christmas Eve, celebrating with strangers, then heading out again Christmas night to celebrate with strangers in a new bar. On one occasion, a friend pitied me enough and invited me to have Christmas dinner at their house. Their warmth saddened me, so I figured I'd just keep drinking until I felt happy. Not only did this strategy not work, I left a horrible impression on the friend's family.

At the end of the day, sobriety will force you to deal with the reasons behind your alcoholism. This might seem obvious, but when you consider that most of us did not start drinking to fix a problem, it's no wonder that this reality alludes us. We started drinking to be the cool kid. Everyone wants to fit in, but for whatever reason, our particular blend of insecurities and personality traits led us down a dark road with alcohol.

The battle against personal insecurity is challenging. Even gaining a small amount of understanding about one's own insecurities is a major victory. Most people don't know themselves or why they behave a certain way. This lack of knowledge is dangerous because of the traps along the way, in which someone might not survive due to learning things the hard way.

You can get drunk to ignore these traps, but you can't hide from them. The simple admission of drinking due to insecurities is a big step. Unfortunately, many people only take this step after a tragic event happens due to their alcohol consumption.

If this letter inspires you to take just one step, evaluate your personal insecurities and how you deal with them. A small amount of awareness can go a long way in the reduction of self-destructive behaviors and the implementation of positive life habits.

Why Do You Drink?

So I've thought about this question a lot. Or rather, I've revisited this question repeatedly over the course of my sobriety. I've come up with different answers, but they're all variations of the same few ideas.

Whether you're a raging alcoholic, a happy hour addict, a frat boy style binge drinker or a weekend warrior, there are many reasons that you can't form a healthy relationship with alcohol.

I want to make something clear: there is no such thing as a *"healthy relationship"* with something that in no way enhances. It would be one thing if alcohol was like a performance-enhancing drug (PED) or was even like methamphetamines (meth).

At worst, PEDs have a significant trade-off. At best, they are extremely safe if used carefully. Meth has a whole list of negatives, but apparently, it gives you quite a bit of energy. I once watched a story about a man who started smoking it to get the energy to run his 2 businesses for 20 hours a day. It worked, but he also got hooked on meth and ended up in prison for 7 years.

Regardless of how much you drink, be aware that you are engaging in an activity with a net negative on your health and well-being. A healthy relationship with it only means that you won't let it destroy you.

With all of this said, the question remains: why do I drink? More specifically, why did I have a relationship with alcohol where it could destroy me?

Addiction

It's said that some people have an *"addictive personality"*. I suppose what this means is that there is something in their genetics that makes them more likely to engage in compulsive behavior. Therefore, it's best to keep them away from destructively and addictive activities like gambling, drinking or drugs.

Do I believe there is such a thing as an addictive personality? Sure. The research points to a combination of biological, psychological and environmental factors that contribute to a person's susceptibility to addiction. Even if I wanted to refute the evidence of various controlled studies, I've enough personal and anecdotal experience to trust the validity of the idea.

I've known people who have gotten addicted to marijuana. Marijuana is supposedly a non-addictive substance, but I've still observed people get hooked on it. Or at the very least, they behaved in a manner that suggested a psychological or physiological dependence on marijuana. On the flip side, I knew a guy who smoked crack on 3 separate occasions and decided he just didn't like it. From a purely biochemical perspective, crack-cocaine is a highly addictive substance. Marijuana isn't. Yet, this occurred.

A behavior neuroscience research study done by the Arizona State University has an excellent definition of addiction *"a brain disorder characterized by compulsive engagement in rewarding stimuli despite adverse consequences."* By this definition, a person can get addicted to anything that offers a rewarding stimulus, even if the end result is destructive.

These substances can include crack-cocaine, heroin, methamphetamine, marijuana and, even food. A person can get addicted to anything. A person can also get addicted to constructive activities as well. My friend, a personal trainer, observed that his hardest working clients were former alcoholics and drug addicts. The same mental malfunction that got them addicted to drugs and alcohol allowed them to get addicted to hard work and success.

I don't believe I have an addictive personality, but this is one of the main reasons many people drink. This is just not the reason I drank. However, I am still an alcoholic. I still have a drinking problem. Once I ruled out the addictive personality, I was able to consider other things.

Lack of Moderation

I don't have a moderation switch. I'm either all in or completely out. Half-assing an activity makes me uncomfortable. This trait was reflected in my drinking style. While some people could sip a drink for hours, I could finish 2-3 martinis or a few pitchers of beer before I even felt a buzz.

I also consume most of my food and non-alcoholic drinks in this manner. I can finish a French press of coffee by myself in under an hour. A person like me must eat healthily and pick constructive things to immerse themselves in, because I don't *"kind of"* do anything.

In most cases, I wasn't drinking to get drunk. I simply don't understand what I'm supposed to do with an empty glass if I'm still thirsty. As a result, I would constantly fill my glass for the very same reason that it was so quickly empty. I lack moderation and approach many things in an obsessive-compulsive manner. This is likely tied to the next major reason I was a heavy drinker.

Boredom

Today, most people's idea of socializing consists of an activity centered around alcohol. In college, it's a house party or themed night at a bar. As an adult, it's happy hour and sporting events. A surprisingly few number of people know how to enjoy themselves without the backdrop of alcohol.

Conversation revolves around sporting events, gossip, and, work. Because most people live for the weekend, they don't have much to discuss outside of these events. At some point, I realized how unfulfilling this was. However, I'm still an extrovert and hadn't matured into being alone. While the socialization wasn't fulfilling, it was better than being alone. Besides, it's not like I didn't enjoy my friends. It's just that the entire bar and club scene was about utility to me.

Either I was there to try to pick up women or I was there to drink. This was the same way I viewed almost every social event as well. I simply didn't enjoy many of the mindless conversations that popped up at house parties or bars. If I didn't have any luck finding a girl, I got drunk as fast as I possibly could.

Loneliness

The unique combination of boredom and an extreme personality is that it makes one feel like an outsider. I was always welcomed by my friends to socialize and drink, but I wasn't particularly happy while out.

I once read that there's a difference between being lonely and alone. I used to think that was a trick of semantics until one night I was at the bar drinking with some friends. These were people I'd known my whole life and I cared deeply about, but I felt lonely.

I felt lonely because this wasn't where I belonged. I didn't know what my scene was at the time, but I knew this environment was not the best use of my time or energy. However, this environment was all that I knew. I didn't dislike it, but I felt like an outsider. To distract myself from this feeling, I drank. Combine this with the two traits previously mentioned—boredom and lack of moderation—and this meant that more often than not, I drank a lot. I never drank to escape any traumatic emotional pain. I drank to pass the time and keep my mind off of how lonely I was. For a period in my life, I lived alone and was relatively isolated. During this time, I drank a nearly a box of wine (About 101 ounces) every 2-3 days. To put that in perspective, there are 128 ounces in a gallon. At my worst, I could easily put away a gallon of wine a day.

I don't think I ever set out to drink so much wine, but it was easy to do it. I was both lonely and alone. Based on this experience, I know that there are some people who are drinking to either numb the feeling of loneliness or to fit in places where they don't naturally conform.

Conditioning

I saved this one for last because I think it's the weakest reason and, therefore, the easiest to deal with. However, that doesn't mean that it isn't a part of the reason myself and so many others drink.

We live in a society that revolves around alcohol consumption. Many of us get to adulthood and can't imagine a social event without alcohol. Drinking is both the right of passage and the cost of entry for people in mainstream society.

Many people will say, *"Oh, you don't have to do what everyone else does. Be your own person."* The people who say this are correct. However, they're correct the same way that I am correct if I say, *"The next time you feel stressed, just play Clair De Lune on the piano."* It'll probably work, but you need a whole host of other skills to be successful with this.

If you know nothing but alcohol in your social functions and family life, then you'll have a difficult time living without it. You may have a drinking problem. You may have problems while drinking. But if everything in your life is related to alcohol, it can be terrifying to do something so different from what you've known. Especially if it's all you've ever known.

Vices To Virtue

Depending on the time you read this, you may or may not have met "Fighter Matt." If you haven't met him yet, just know that he's going to be a great a friend with a ton of real life experience which was gained the hard way. The bad news is that he will become one of your favorite drinking partners. For nearly five years, you two will be notorious for your epic levels of drinking and the trouble you get in to.

However, in 2011, while you're living in L.A., Matt decides he's had enough and gets sober. You meet up with him one day, fully expecting him to lecture you on the values of sobriety and why I should also stop drinking. Instead, he gives you a remarkable piece of advice disguised as an impeccably timed proverb of wisdom.

> "The very thing that made you a heavy drinker will make you great at whatever else you decide to do."

At the time, Matt's statement didn't make much sense. At best, it was some type of cryptic kaon whose meaning would only be discovered a few years later. At worst, you thought it was a meaningless play on words. It's not until your third year of sobriety that you came to understand and experience the meaning behind these words.

I remember the moment clearly: I was out watching a football game with some friends and I became aware of how bored I was. The environment wasn't interesting and I didn't care about the game. I just wanted to get home, sip some tea, and get back to work on my book. When I was drinking, I would have ordered another drink to numb myself to the changes in my mood. With that no longer an option, I said my goodbyes and went home to immerse myself in a project I was working on.

Drinking was my default response to boredom. I've never had a problem keeping myself entertained. I don't mind being alone and I don't mind remaining silent in a group because I can always find ways to occupy myself.

As an alcoholic, my preferred way to do this was alcohol consumption. Now that I'm sober, I leave and do something more interesting elsewhere. This seems simple, but it's amazing what trouble a person will let themselves get into when facing boredom and insecurity.

Certain triggers motivate you to drink, which later makes you crave more. As a result, you begin to see drinking as the best option for entertainment. It's a cycle that is difficult to break and the primary reason you must change your environment to get sober.

If for some reason leaving is not an option, then I will read on my phone or think deeply about problems I need to solve. In the instance of attending family functions where it's impolite to leave early, I've learned to bring a notebook to write ideas and thoughts I'm having at the moment.

I've always understood how to entertain myself. Since most of the socializing at the bar bored me, I passed the time by drinking. Sometimes I drank heavily. Sometimes I drank slowly. However, I always drank excessively because I was drinking to fill the time. Sobriety forced me to recognize this and create a new solution. I didn't have to alleviate boredom through alcohol. I could simply leave the bar.

There was also another reason that I drank heavily: I tend to fixate on matters and lack moderation in my pursuit of conquest. This ultimately results in an unbalanced manner of consumption. This is yet another crippling vice that I was able to transform into a supportive virtue.

For example, I simply don't understand the purpose of talking over a nice meal. I'd rather quickly consume the meal and talk afterwards; or simply not meet for a meal at all and instead have coffee. I don't enjoy small talk and much of dinner and socializing is filled with exactly that.

This is not to say that I don't understand and cannot abide by social conventions. I just don't enjoy some of them. I used to drink alcohol to endure them, but now I just drink tea or coffee. These social conventions have also forced me to become a better conversationalist and learn to better connect with people to pass the time. Sobriety has given me the ability to apply my compulsions to other more constructive areas of my life.

Rather than apply this tendency to alcohol, I apply it to knowledge acquisition. I'm better at focusing on and solving problems. I'd rather sit in one place and work incessantly to finish something than take it easy and break it down. I'm excellent at completing huge chunks of work without a break, as I believe this allows me to gain momentum and focus better. Rather than be a victim of inertia, I've learned to use momentum to accomplish work.

The channeling of obsessive energy is what makes someone a great success or a miserable failure. You see, many people believe that the biggest losers are the ones who do nothing with their lives. This feels intuitively correct but proves to be false upon closer inspection.

Although doing nothing won't get you far, it also won't tremendously hold you back. How terrible an existence can you really have if you do nothing but go to work, come home, consume alcohol, and play video games? You won't achieve anything great, but you also won't do anything tragic.

Prisons are not full of people who did nothing. Life-changing decisions are not made by idle losers. Instead, they're made by people who are trying to do something. They're made by the obsessed individuals who misdirect and misapply their energy.

Every mistake I made and problem I had while intoxicated did not happen because I was sitting on my couch with a six-pack of beer every night. While that would not be an optimal existence, it's not an existence which causes many issues. Many of my problems occurred because I was trying to do something rather than nothing.

I wanted to be the biggest partier and drinker that people knew. This obsession stemmed from my loneliness and insecurity. Many people want approval, but they lack the resolve to go after what they want. Of all the problems I had, the inability to take action was not one of them. This was yet another way my strongest traits were channeled towards the most destructive route.

I've always prided myself on going after what I want and doing what it takes to get it. When I thought the best way to be liked was by being a loud, outspoken, womanizing drunk, this is what I did. I now seek approval by being an outstanding example to others around me.

I fixate on work which will make a difference and impact people's lives. Feeling motivated and driven to work all night to produce a great piece of writing (and thus earn people's admiration) is as natural to me as it was to stay out drinking until 2AM to impress people.

This is what my friend Matt meant when he said:

> "The very thing that made you a heavy drinker will make you great at whatever else you decide to do [when you're sober]."

The very personality trait which was once a vice can be turned into a virtue. Just as your vices took you to your lowest point, your virtues can elevate you to your highest point.

The Never Ending Guilt

Growing up, I was a big fan of the show Buffy: The Vampire Slayer and its spin-off, Angel. If you aren't familiar, *"Buffy: The Vampire Slayer"* was about a girl named Buffy gifted with super-strength and aided by powerful companions who, as the name suggests, kills vampires. Rather than kill all of them, she makes friends with some and even falls in love with one named Angel. Eventually, Angel was given his own series where he battled vampires as well as various other supernatural creatures.

Angel's difference from other vampires is what makes him interesting. In the mythology of the series, vampires lack a soul. According to the show, the soul gives humans their ability to feel the emotions of empathy and guilt. Because vampires lack a soul, they're able to ruthlessly kill and feel no remorse for their actions. In fact, the vampires in the show enjoy tormenting and torturing their victims before killing them.

> *"Killing is so merciful at the end, isn't it? The pain has ended."*
> -Angelus

Angel roamed the Earth as a vampire without a soul until one day he was cursed by a clan of gypsies. He remained a vampire but was given the burden of a soul. At this point, he began to harbor extreme guilt and became deeply remorseful for all the killings he'd done as a soulless vampire. All the bad feelings and apprehensions he should have felt over the years would now haunt him. Since vampires are immortal, he was doomed to spend the rest of his existence wracked with guilt and regret over who he was and the things he'd done.

There are times when my sobriety makes me feel like Angel. Though it may seem silly, I see a lot of myself in the mythology of this character. The altered state of mind does not excuse the people you hurt and the damage you cause under the influence, but it's only during sobriety that you're able to comprehend the extent of and empathize with the effect of your intoxicated actions. In talking with other recovering alcoholics, this guilt appears so often that I gave it a name: *"Angelus Syndrome"*.

In the series, Angel is short for *"Angelus"*. Angelus Syndrome is an appropriate name because you only experience the guilt once a fundamental change occurs. Angel did not feel bad for the killing until he became, at his core, a new being. Only then was he able to consider the effect of his past actions with a new conscience. Regardless of how bad you feel about something you did after another night of heavy drinking, it will pale in comparison to what you feel once you've made the decision to get sober.

The sober mind can analyze the past with clarity, and the sober heart can truly experience empathy. When your life is under the influence of alcohol, you behave destructively towards yourself, your friends, and your environment because your heart is drowned in alcohol. Less poetically, it's been demonstrated that alcohol greatly distorts your ability to evaluate and respond to the emotional reactions of people around you.

In a February 2013 study published by Alcoholism: Clinical and Experimental Research, it was revealed that *"Chronic alcohol abuse seems to have effects on the perception and decoding of emotional expressions."*

The researcher went on to say that *"It has been associated with higher frequencies of alexithymia, meaning deficits in emotion recognition and verbalization, leading to difficulties in distinguishing and comprehending people's emotional states, and then using emotional information to plan social and interactive acts."*

This research says, in academic language, what drinkers know from experience: alcohol causes you to misread, misinterpret, and incorrectly respond to the subtle and obvious social clues. Intoxication makes you an asshole without a soul.

For all intents and purposes, alcohol has broken your heart and mind. Like a broken bone, your mental and emotional faculties require time and protection to heal from trauma. Each time you get drunk, you're restarting the clock for how much time you need to heal.

For the alcoholic, each drunken episode is striking the bone before it heals. Not only will it remain broken, but it becomes even further distorted, disfigured, and dysfunctional. When you're an alcoholic who has yet to begin recovery, you are simply unable to understand, appreciate, and coordinate your actions.

Once you stop drinking, then you start healing. Your mind and heart gradually begin to function correctly again. While this is good for many things, it makes you brutally aware of your past behavior with an intensity that you are not prepared for. This is the guilt that Angelus could only feel once he had gotten a soul. This is the guilt an alcoholic can only feel once they become sober.

How You See Yourself Before You Get Sober

While I was still drinking, I never felt guilty for anything I did while drinking. No matter how big an asshole I was, how many risks I took, or how often I got behind the wheel, I never felt bad about any of it. I'd regret doing something if I didn't get what I wanted out of it, but I never felt remorse for my actions while I was an alcoholic.

Based on everything I know now, it's probably more accurate to say that I was incapable of feeling guilt. I don't state it like this to alleviate responsibility—only to highlight how much damage alcohol can do to your ability to emotionally connect with another human. Once your conscience is under the influence of alcohol, and your ability to properly analyze a situation is compromised, you inevitably become self-centered and self-serving.

Alcoholism turned me into a narcissistic, selfish, sociopath.

Occasionally, I felt bad, but it was only if I caused genuine harm or offense. Even then, it was short lived and insincere. For example, I felt terrible if I insulted a friend; yet, to say that I experienced guilt wouldn't be quite right. To be more accurate, I knew that I did something repulsive that had the potential to get me ostracized and I wanted people to quickly forget it.

Moreover, I wanted to move past it and get back to self-serving fun.

A broken conscience is a self-perpetuating monster. Even though you know that you're wrong, you try to push past the feelings and ignore it. Or you try to extinguish your feelings with alcohol so that you can conveniently blame everything on the alcohol. This further damages your conscience and makes you more likely to engage in a selfish and destructive behavior.

I relied on alcohol as a justification when my drunk behavior got out of control. I figured that if I blamed my conduct on drinking, everything would be alright. I also convinced myself that if I gave things enough time, everyone would eventually have a good laugh about the situation.

Unfortunately, people have surprisingly long memories, especially when you engage in behaviors they disapprove of. Even after I was banned from social events and my reputation earned an irreparable black eye, I didn't really feel guilty about my drinking.

Rather than feel bad, I blamed other people for being overly sensitive. If they couldn't forgive and forget my intoxicated behavior, I saw them as hypocrites. This hypocrisy would anger me and lead to a cruel irony; I became angry with others because of their response to my degenerate behavior.

Although this changed when I got sober, I didn't immediately feel guilty. It took some time before my mind was repaired enough to analyze the past and for my heart to be mended enough to feel the effects of it. However, when I had the first flashback of my drunken behavior through the lens of sobriety, I nearly wept.

It's only when you stop drinking that you can objectively consider the effect you've had on your environment. A mental analysis of what you've done is not complicated. All that is required is an understanding of cause and effect. This occurs relatively fast. The emotional impact and the accompanying guilt are not only delayed, but it forever haunts you with undulating intensity. This only starts to hit you once you've spent enough time sober.

It's as if alcoholism consumes your soul. However, your soul does not instantly return the moment you stop drinking. Only after discipline and dedication will you regain enough of it to experience guilt. As Angel was called *"The Vampire with a Soul,"* you become *"The Alcoholic with A Soul."*

The Alcoholic With A Soul

Guilt is a poor catalyst for sobriety because many people drink to deal with their emotions, and guilt is one of those emotions. At times I drank because I felt guilty. Sometimes I felt guilty because I drank. Either way, guilt is the forever loyal drinking partner of the alcoholic. It serves as an enabler rather than a deterrent.

The longer I'm sober, the less I experience guilt attacks about the past. Nevertheless, Angelus Syndrome never fully dissipates. Like a herpes infection on my conscience, it goes into remission and stays hidden for years, but certain events trigger the embarrassing memories of my past. At these moments, waves of guilt crash into me and force self-reflection.

As of this writing, I've only been sober for five years. However, I've asked other people who have been sober longer than I about these powerful guilt trips and if they ever fully dissipate. They tell me that the guilt never fades, but this is not a bad thing. The guilt reminds you of how much ruin you brought upon yourself and to others. It serves as a powerful reminder of how bad it was and it motivates you to never let it get that way again. Guilt can be your greatest asset for staying faithful to your sobriety.

The guilt also allows you to develop compassion for the other side. Most of us only know sobriety from the drinker's perspective. Many drinkers—alcoholic or not—harbor a silent judgment of people who aren't drinking. They feel mildly uneasy and slightly threatened by the presence of a teetotaler.

If you doubt this, consider how uncomfortable most people feel when trying to socialize without a drink. Even the presence of non-drinkers makes many drinkers uncomfortable to the point where they ask, *"Why aren't you drinking?"* Alcohol is the only drug where people assume you have a problem if you don't use it.

At best, non-drinkers are assumed to be the designated drivers of the group. At worst, drinkers hurl derogatory epithets at those who choose not to imbibe with the goal of pressuring them into drinking. Once you experience the sober side of this, you understand how repulsive and obnoxious this behavior makes you.

This new perspective develops deep sympathy within you for people who have endured this aspect of your drunken behavior. You are now looking at the drinker's world through the lens of sobriety.

Guilt Allows You To Experience The World Like Most People

Alcoholic guilt allows you to see that many people can drink without destroying themselves and their surroundings. If you use the guilt correctly, you will see just how different you are—not only from sober people but also from other drinkers.

You realize that the excuses you used don't ease the hurt caused or the undo the damage inflicted. Just because the time passed a certain way for you doesn't mean that others have moved on. Maybe see things one way, but other people see matters differently. You may have regained your soul, but there is nothing you can do about the past.

I've yet to discover a remedy for this guilt. Even though I've forgiven myself, the guilt has not gone away; this is probably a good thing. I have enjoyed the benefits of sobriety too much to even consider drinking again. However, the guilt serves as a powerful deterrent should I ever reconsider my position.

The guilt increases my compassion and understanding of others. Even though the decision to quit drinking is executed in an instant, the planning that goes into it feels like it takes a lifetime. I understand the fear and apprehension which accompanies making a drastic lifestyle change. This is why I never pressure anyone to stop drinking. However, if someone is thinking about it and voices their concerns to me, I speak their language—regardless of which substance they're addicted to.

Lastly, my guilt allows me to remain humble and grateful. One of the reasons I have such guilt is because my life turned out well. I never got in trouble with the law, I just barely kept all my close friends, I'm in a great relationship, and I've served as a great inspiration to others rather than a terrible warning. Many times, I feel undeserving of my situation and the people in my life.

This is the power of guilt; it can make sure that you remain appreciative of what you have, despite your past thoughts and actions. Regaining your soul and uniting with your conscience is powerful. It prevents you from drifting back to the other side and becoming the self-destructive monster you've worked hard to leave behind.

There is a part of the Angel mythology I left out. After Angelus got his soul back, he tried to continue his old ways. However, his new soul and conscience prevented this. He exiles himself from the world, wallowing in self-pity and guilt until he decides to help rid the world of the type of evil he once was.

These letters are my way of exterminating the evil that I once was. I know I cannot change the past, so sobriety is my way of making sure I don't repeat it. I'm not sure if my heart and mind are completely repaired, but I know they're functional enough to generate guilt when I think about my past. I can sympathize and empathize with people going through similar struggles.

These letters give me a chance to help someone cause less damage to themselves, the world, and to regain a soul.

Regrets And What You Think You're Missing

When you leave what you've always known, there is no way to escape the feeling of *"missing out"*. For the majority of my 20s, the only way I knew how to socialize or meet women was through the bar, clubbing, and heavy drinking culture. One of my great fears about getting sober is that I'd lose out on a social life and that all my friends would forget about me.

On my first day of sobriety, after I left my first AA meeting, the first thing I did was send a mass text message to my closest friends informing them of my decision. I don't remember exactly what I said, but it went approximately like this:

I asked for their support and I told them I was scared, but I did not specify of exactly what. At that moment I wasn't exactly sure what I feared, but I eventually came to realize that I was terrified of two things: the past and future.

The present moment made me feel empowered and excited because I was making a choice about my life. Taking back control of their life and applying themselves to a path of self-improvement makes most people feel positive—even if it's only in the moment. The feeling persists even if they eventually give up or revert to their old habits. For the moment, I was optimistic.

I feared the past because it's done and I knew that my behavior was less than exemplary. There was nothing I could do to fix what I'd done, mute what I had said, or erase what I'd written. People remember how an action made them feel far more than the exact details of its execution. I feared the future because I didn't want to go back to who I was.

I was worried that I lacked the strength or the willpower to stay committed to my goal. While I had the optimism and gusto that comes with setting a new goal, I was worried that I'd eventually let myself down. The thought of being the same person 5 years later was a terrifying prospect.

My other big fear is that I would be missing out on socializing and bonding. I've since come to learn that true bonds of friendship are not dependent on the number of happy hours that you hit together. However, when this is all you've known for the better part of a decade, this is a reasonable fear. I believe that many alcoholics know they need sobriety, but they need people more and, in their minds, the two goals directly clash with one another.

I wish I could say that this fear goes away after a few months of keeping in touch with your friends and seeing that nothing changes. This would be a blatant lie. Rather than dissipate with time and subtle reassurance, it intensifies as your worst fears slowly manifest themselves. You won't exactly lose your friends, but sobriety causes such a shift in your perception and reality that it's impossible to live life as it was before you got sober.

You'll spend less time with your friends who drink because a significant portion of socializing is drinking. It's not a good idea for a person new to sobriety to spend time in a drinking environment. Whether you learn this the easy way or the hard way depends on your personality, but the nature of your social interactions will change because you've changed.

This isn't negative. It's just new. Think of it this way: if you and your friends were fat and you decided to get in shape, you'd have to stop doing things that made you fat. Since your friends are still engaging in that lifestyle, you will—by both necessity and practicality—stop spending time with them.

You no longer engage in the activities that many of them do. There doesn't have to be any love lost between you all, but it's inevitable that you will spend less time with old friends.

Since the fear doesn't disappear, your only option is to develop the resolve to push forward despite your apprehensions and reservations. This is only possible when fear of returning to the pain of your past outweighs your fear of losing your future comradery. There is more power in avoiding pain than preserving pleasure. Understanding this will not only allow you to get sober but will give you the ability to adhere to any major life changes you may make.

Future Projection Erases Momentary Regrets

"You have been down there, Neo. You know that road. You know exactly where it ends. And I know that's not where you want to be."
-Trinity, The Matrix

The quote above is from a scene in the movie *"The Matrix"*. Neo has yet to step into the Matrix and is confronted with a moment of choice: Push forward into the unknown in pursuit of what he's always wanted, or return to the familiar yet mediocre where he knows he isn't fulfilling his potential.

When I first saw the Matrix as a 12-year-old, I just thought it was a cool sci-fi movie with great fight scenes. I didn't grasp the philosophical brilliance of the movie for another decade and a half when I started to make major changes in how I was living.

I thought about all that I was potentially missing out on—good times with my friends, delicious alcoholic beverages, nights out socializing, and the chance to unwind at the end of a busy day. These were the *"positives"*. I was so afraid of being separated from my safety net of familiarity, that the loss of the things delayed my decision to get sober by almost 4 years.

When we think about making a major change, we tend to only focus on what we're losing rather than what we're gaining or—more importantly— what will happen if we continue on the same path.

Good times with my friends took time away from developing myself into a better person. Alcoholic beverages are delicious, but that makes it easier to spend money and consume more of them. Nights out socializing gave me temporary fun, but took away from getting closer to my goals. I never drank to unwind. It was always to numb myself to my failures and give myself a temporary boost of importance.

The truth is that I was a barely tolerable nobody with minimum value who was only tolerated by people I considered to be friends. Living daily as this person pissed me off. I was on a fast track to lonely Loserville, and drinking helped me escape from how this made me feel. If I wanted to get my life together, I knew that I would have to stop drinking. I didn't know exactly what my future held, but I knew that sobriety was the key to getting there because severe and frequent intoxication is what I reasoned was holding me back.

Even if I didn't know exactly who I'd become or what my place in the world would be, I'd already been down the other road and I knew exactly where it ended. It wasn't where I wanted to be. Suddenly, all the things

I thought I was missing out on seemed foolish to worry over. My fear of being a washed up, lonely, self-medicating loser is what allowed me to finally accept these fears and take action.

This fear made me selfish. Selfishness gets a bad reputation, but that's only if you use it to unnecessarily cause other people harm or inconvenience. I realized that I did not care about myself enough before, so rather than invest in myself and control my drinking, I squandered my time, abilities, and reputation. My priorities were so out of order that I believed it was more important to be popular than to build financial security. Even now, it's unclear as to whether alcohol was the cause or the effect of these delusions, but it's obvious that it played a central role.

Future projection is a powerful tool for changing your life. The act of sitting down and considering the most likely outcome of continuing along a certain path is invaluable. I'd done this several times before getting sober and came to grim conclusions. Occasionally I saw a future where I was some type of romantic figure who was always drunk but wildly successful, but these were flights of fantasy. Sure, that could happen, but the most likely outcome was that of me ending up in prison, homeless, or lonely.

Despite that, I didn't quit drinking because I didn't care. Having a goal is powerful, but it's useless if you don't want more for yourself. Nowhere in my experiences or searches have I found a way to motivate people to want more or do better. Nowhere in these letters do I claim that I can do that or that it's possible. However, I do believe that many people simply haven't reached the point where the fear of regression outweighs the comfort of stagnation. I believe it's possible to get someone to that point faster or channel it to get keep them going, but if they enjoy being an underachiever, there's nothing that any external influence can do.

I didn't care about being a scumbag, and that's the truth. I just figured that if people didn't like me, it was their fault and we wouldn't get along sober anyway. Then I looked at what I had accomplished so far in my life at that time, and how I felt when I looked at myself in the mirror. Deep down, I believed I was better than how I'd been behaving. I believed that I had more potential than what I had manifested so far. I knew that I could be more than clinging to the past relationships and old habits that were holding me back.

Actually, I didn't really believe any of this—at least not so much that I had unshakable confidence in the outcome and believed I was destined for greatness. There was no reason to think this. I lied to myself and started to act as if it were true, because I was terrified of where the road

I was on lead to. If lying to myself was the only way off that path, then I would lie to myself. By attempting to make the lie true, it eventually became a reality.

This is how you move past your old fears and future regrets about the things you'll miss out on. Imagine the way your life would be if you keep this up, then lie to yourself that you deserve better. Even if you know it's a lie, your fear of the life you'll have if you continue down the old road will make you behave in a way that makes the lie reality.

Before you know it, you'll be in a position where you don't mind looking at yourself in the mirror. You don't fear losing the old friends if you change. By turning off that dark road to nowhere, you give yourself no choice but to head towards the light and become a person you love and respect.

One Day At A Time

To expect instantaneous healing after being broken for such a long time is foolish. Furthermore, harboring this expectation only discourages you. Change doesn't happen overnight. Only by taking matters one day at a time will you finally get your life in order.

I always remind people that you must take it one day at a time. People forget that the more valuable something is, the longer it takes to obtain. All the best things in life are a function of time. We often fail to appreciate this, and when we do, it is the cause of unnecessary hardship and tremendous misery.

When it's time to wait, we become impatient. When it's time to be strong, we become weak. When it's obvious that the old way of doing things is ineffective, we stubbornly cling to the past. Impatience, weakness, and aversion to change are the worst enemies of sobriety. The only way to conquer them and enjoy a sober life is by slowing down, staying strong, being willing to change, and taking things one day at a time.

When I first stopped drinking, I counted the days. After 30 days passed, I counted the months. After 12 months, I counted the years. I anticipate this book will be published between my 4th and 5th years of sobriety. To make it this far, I've battled with the three-headed beast and emerged victorious so far. My plan is to continue this winning streak and reap the benefits that come with sustained victory.

As a result, I know these enemies well. I know that you'll encounter them on your journey to sobriety. Learn well about them so that you can have the best chance of success. After all, an enemy you can't see is an enemy you can't attack.

Impatience

Impatience is the first enemy of your sobriety. The first few times I tried to get sober, I expected to wake up and feel like a million bucks the very next day. Moreover, I expected people to admire my decision and anticipated that their congratulations would instantly wash my guilt away. I thought that my life would suddenly improve, the bad memories would vanish, and I would be instantly forgiven.

A few of my attempts to stop drinking were motivated by extreme guilt. I remember a time where a group of people who I regarded as friends were warning potential dates about my drunken behavior. My reaction at the moment was to feel betrayed and angry, but I was also embarrassed and I knew that I earned this treatment. If people felt motivated enough to warn a stranger about how I acted, then I clearly had a problem.

At that moment, I decided to stop drinking because I felt terrible. While sobriety was a good idea for me regardless, I did it because I wanted instant relief from the discomfort that this recent revelation brought me.

I don't remember how long my discomfort lasted, but I do recall being drunk the very next week on a beach. There is a lack of discipline and commitment here, but part of this was my impatience and pursuit of instant gratification. I expected the opinions of people who issued warnings about me to change overnight. Since they did not, I did not change when I should I have.

Getting sober is only the first step of a long, arduous journey. Due to years of self-destructive behavior, my health and habits were atrocious. This, coupled with the late nights and caffeine-fueled early mornings, took an incredible toll on my body. I didn't sleep when I was tired and I was tired when I should have had energy.

Sleep is vital to maintaining a healthy mental and emotional state. Chronic alcohol abuse disrupts sleep and so it follows that your physical, mental, and emotional health is disrupted as well. The cruel reality is that these disruptions not only make it more difficult to stop drinking, they also make you more likely to abuse alcohol.

I am not telling you this to discourage you. You'll feel better, probably sooner than you expect, but you won't feel better immediately. You'll have to take it one day at a time.

Weakness

Weakness is the second enemy of your sobriety. You have a problem, and if you're trying to get sober, you've finally admitted this to yourself. Do not underestimate the difficulty of admitting to yourself that you have a problem. Admitting that you are an alcoholic, by definition, means you lack the strength necessary to control your consumption of alcohol. The sooner you can admit this to yourself, the better off you'll be.

I didn't take the process of recovery seriously for almost 3 years because I believed that my behavior was normal. Society enforced it, my immediate environment enforced it, and my closest friends enforced it. My friends aren't bad people. In fact, they gave me tremendous support when I began to take my recovery seriously, but you must remember something: very few people are able to spot the signs of alcoholism. Even fewer are bold enough to confront you about it—especially if they regularly drink with you.

I will reference this point several times throughout these letters because it's important for you to understand. Most people will not be told they have an alcohol problem by an external entity. People are afraid of appearing to be hypocrites or being accused of ruining the fun. It will be up to you to admit to yourself that you have a problem and stick by your decision to do something about it.

Of course, no one takes your decision seriously until you do. This greatly surprised me, however, it is human nature. Although I expected the world to honor my decision, it didn't until I did.

The younger you are, the fewer people will believe in your sobriety. This problem is partially attributed to the common, wanton claims to get sober most people make after a rough night of drinking. This phenomenon has become a meme of young adult behavior. During my first few attempts at sobriety, I partially believed that my social circle would implicitly honor my decision by not having booze around and not offering it to me.

Our general society, your environment, and your closest friends will try to convince you that you don't have a problem. However, you know how you feel and whether or not you have an unhealthy relationship with alcohol. The first time you ask yourself if you're an alcoholic, it's likely an overreaction to a rough night. The second time you ask this question, it's cause for alarm. By the time you ask yourself this the third time, it's too late. Now is the time for you to be strong. Your health, reputation, and life depend on it.

Stubbornness

Aversion to change is the third enemy of your sobriety. By definition, it is also the most difficult one for people to overcome. Abstaining from alcohol is not what's difficult about sobriety. I've met many alcoholics and very few feel a legitimate craving for a drink. There are a surprising number of treatments to help people who have developed a physical dependency on alcohol. Yet, even if these people took the treatment, they'd still be up against the biggest challenge of sobriety: your own worst tendencies and refusal to change.

You're not addicted to the taste of alcohol or even how it makes you feel. You're addicted to the common rituals and practices of drinking. To you, sobriety is more than just not consuming alcohol. It represents the dismantling of everything you know about relating to the world around you.

As social creatures, humans don't do well with prolonged periods of isolation. Even the most devoted misanthropist needs to be around people at times. This desire is even stronger in younger people who are most likely to be out drinking as part of the typical social routine we're indoctrinated into from high school.

Social events in this society are so reliant on alcohol that people feel the need to specify whether or not an event is *"dry"*. Sobriety will distance you from many social events. Many people can't navigate the new life they must lead so they don't bother starting (even though they know they should) or they drive themselves back to alcohol because of the isolation they experience. It's easier to resist change than it is to build a new identity.

Persistence Over Time Is The Only Thing That Works

Sobriety does not mend a broken life any more than a cast mends a broken bone. It is merely the first step in recovering from the damage which wrecked, misaligned, and malfunctioned your life.

While I do not believe that recovery is a process that lasts your entire life, I do feel that it takes as long as anything worth acquiring. Generally speaking, the best things in life are a function of time. Getting sober is no different.

Sobriety requires a commitment to a goal that runs counter to the agenda of the most powerful industries in society who profit from your alcohol consumption. It's not an accident that it is so difficult to change your habits and lifestyle if you want to stop drinking. Marketers do their best to ensure that you continue spending money on their product, and the legal system loves when you get in trouble and must pay to fix it. As a result, society and the pressure it exerts on you is an opponent of your sobriety.

I hope these challenges inspire you. If you know that the task you face is difficult but necessary to your success, you are more likely to engage it with the seriousness it deserves. If you don't believe it's important, you won't try. I already know that you believe sobriety is important. Your reading of these letters is evidence of that.

If you don't believe it's challenging, you will not summon your full faculties to take it on. You will rush, you will falter, and you will refuse to do the steps. Whether it be out of arrogance, laziness, or hubris, you will do what it takes to free yourself from the destructive effects of alcohol. But if you respect this problem and you truly want your mind, body, and soul back, you'll diligently take things one day at a time.

> "Permanence, perseverance, and persistence in spite of all obstacles, discouragements, and impossibilities: It is this, that in all things distinguishes the strong soul from the weak."
>
> -Thomas Carlyle (4 December 1795 – 5 February 1881)
> Scottish philosopher, satirical writer, essayist, translator, historian, mathematician, and teacher

Monsters Beneath the Surface

I used to say that occasionally getting blackout drunk was necessary to ensure that I was right in the head. My reasoning was that being blackout drunk removed all the filters from my communication and action. Just typing these words feels incredibly stupid, but at the time I thought this was an excellent way to learn about what lurked beneath the surface of my conscious mind.

One function of human consciousness is to control self-destructive desires. These monsters beneath the surface may last for a moment. They may last for days. They may even last for a lifetime. However, they do not define us because they reside in the subconscious. Fortunately, we are judged on our conscious actions rather than our subconscious thoughts.

Although my analysis was correct, my reasoning was flawed. Humans have many horrible, disgusting, deceitful thoughts, all of which are motivated by selfish desires. Aside from the damage to your physical body, getting blackout drunk is dangerous because it removes the guardian of these monstrous motivations. In this heavily inebriated state of mind, these subconscious thoughts are now free to impose their will on your conscious reality and this never ends well.

At best, your personality becomes annoying but harmless. If you have a strong, deeply ingrained value system, you're unlikely to harm yourself or those around you. Your friends would prefer that you don't drink, but at the end of the day, a little liver damage and a rough night of sleep is the only discomfort you endure.

However, the reality is much worse. The monsters in your subconscious escape every time. Things you used to control are now free to express themselves. The result of this is never good. These monsters include: envy of friends, the lust towards their girlfriends, inferiority complexes, personal insecurities, resentment over things you can't let go, and sadness over issues you thought you had forgotten.

The escape of dark, subconscious thoughts are why otherwise peaceful individuals become violent after consuming too much alcohol. They know better than to fight people while they're sober. However, the violence which is usually kept in check manages to break free while under the influence.

Your self-control vanishes after a certain amount of alcohol. Each drop lures the conscious gatekeeper further and further away until the guard against the worst features of your personality is gone. The old saying is that *"The poison is in the dosage"*. This principle is especially relevant about alcohol.

In another note, I listed the differences between the two types of alcoholics: those with drinking problems and those who have problems while drinking. The removal of the conscious gatekeeper is the main reason behind the issues of the latter group.

Some people do not want their lesser nature to reveal itself. These people range from good people with strong values but a few personal issues to those who are aware but refuse to indulge in alcohol because they know something is lurking beneath the surface.

The other end of the spectrum is more insidious. These individuals are searching for ways to indulge their bestial nature. They want an excuse to be the worst version of themselves, and alcohol is the most convenient alibi.

Many people do not understand why they become offensive fools while under the influence, but they know it happens. Intimate knowledge of a phenomenon is not necessary to understand how to manipulate it or to avoid the consequences of misusing it. You don't need to be an electrical engineer to turn on a light switch or avoid the consequences of sticking a fork into a power outlet.

We fail to comprehend the power of secondary effects regarding the escape of subconscious monsters. These secondary effects are haunting, even during sobriety. They leave footprints on the sober(,) conscious mind, and they remain long after the monsters have retreated back into the recesses of your mind.

I am not a mental health professional. I am merely drawing on personal experiences; these experiences have allowed me to reach reasonable, albeit shocking, conclusions. Despite our levels of consciousness, we know that our undesirable traits are self-destructive and, therefore, looked down upon. This negative reinforcement weakens our desire to indulge in our worst behaviors.

Even while we are under the influence of alcohol, we still "know" that we shouldn't do certain things. When we slip up, we feel bad because the rules of society say we ought to. Whether you like it or not, an external moral compass is responsible for the many reasons why we do not behave badly.

However, when society excuses or encourages drunken behavior, something destructive happens. The monsters that lurk beneath the surface are no longer shunned. They are greeted with a smile and encouraged to come forth. The encouraging welcome increases the monster's strength. As a result, the monsters require less and less alcohol to creep out of the subconscious.

This warm welcome motivates the conscious mind to more frequently invite the monsters out to play. Consider the following: people are bolder and more talkative when they drink. Even the most introverted and reticent person can become the outgoing and talkative life of the party. They would never behave in this manner without the influence of alcohol (or some other mind-altering substance).

When they do, they are rewarded with social validation and acceptance. If they enjoy those feelings, but only know how to behave this way with the assistance of alcohol, they'll be more inclined to drink.

This social openness is a trait that is generally considered positive. It manifests as a result of alcohol's mitigating effect on the barrier separating the conscious and subconscious; drinking allows people to *"get out of their head"*. The problem is that when the barrier is down, both positive and negative traits are allowed to express themselves. If your demons are welcomed, excused, or even tolerated, you will more frequently seeks ways to express this behavior.

You may even try to become this darker version of yourself when you aren't drinking. If you let the monsters out regularly enough, distinguishing between your conscious mind and your subconscious desires becomes impossible. Frequently removing the gatekeepers eliminates their desire to stand watch. As more of your lower self escapes, the more your higher self will be eroded.

The destruction of your conscious personality occurs gradually, but eventually the speed will increase. I've watched this happen to myself and other individuals. Once the monsters gain enough ground, they will not willingly retreat without drastic behavioral changes.

I Know Who I Am. Who Are You?

I think about who you are right now. The person you are right now has no idea what you're going to become. Sure, you have hopes and aspirations, but you doubt your ability to get there. You know that your current lifestyle isn't sustainable, your relationships must mature, your bad habits must die, and you must make progress. Logically, you understand this. Intellectually, you know that you are capable. Realistically, you know that despite your best efforts in the past, you have already failed many times.

I'm writing to you from the future to let you know that we do get past the problems with alcohol and the issues that come with it. Though we're separated in time and space, I know who I am, I know who you are, and I know that you will make it from there to here.

I am happy how things turn out. To say that I have no regrets would be foolish. What is more accurate to say is that while I'm grateful for the lessons, I wish that I could have gotten them a different way. I don't regret the outcome. I regret the process. I know that you'll get through it, but it's going to be a challenge. I know you can do it because you are me, and I know who I am.

I know the place you're at in your life and I know what you're thinking: *"Who is this guy? This can't be me. I can't believe I'm ever going to get sober, clean up my life, and go on to be an upstanding citizen. Buddy, I know who I am. Who are you?"*

Your disbelief is sensible. I won't try to talk you out of it. We both know that it's impossible to make someone believe something positive about themselves if they aren't ready to accept it. This is a most depressing aspect of human nature. You think that you can do these things, but you don't yet believe you can do them.

What I'll do instead is demonstrate that it's inevitable that you'll make the positive changes. It's easier for me to prove this to you than to convince you of it. I know that I can't change our timeline, nor do I really want to. The value of the path is not found in the destination. It's found on the journey and often involves mistakes. My hope is that by demonstrating to you how we get here, you can show this letter to someone as an inspiration who doesn't believe they will get past a tough phase.

There are other challenges in life that people doubt that they can get past. What I'm about to show you will also work for those challenges. All that is required is a genuine desire for improvement. If that's in place, everything else will work.

The Inevitable Path to Improvement

Nothing lasts forever. All actions have a finite energy source. When that source of energy is exhausted, one of two things must occur: you cease the action or put more energy into it. This is a simple law of the universe that applies to all actions, whether they're positive or negative. Nothing can persist or last forever.

First, the bad news. This means that your good habits require constant upkeep. Over time, you'll exert less energy, but it doesn't mean that good habits are ironclad safeguards against the bad. They're a line of defense. That's all. That line requires upkeep and vigilance to remain effective at protecting you.

The good news is that bad habits aren't an automatic death sentence. They require energy and upkeep as well. What this means is that assuming they don't kill you, you'll get tired of certain destructive habits you have. This is no guarantee that you won't reload on the energy it takes to sustain them. It just means that they become more difficult to attain the same enjoyment and benefit out of them.

It's draining and difficult because you will get tired of the repercussions. You will get tired of pissing people off, enduring the financial stress that results from wasting your money on alcohol, and dodging encounters with the law. The social support system for your bad habits, in the form of enabling friends, also falls out. Without friends who tag along, you're forced to make some simple but profound decisions.

You'll start projecting yourself into the future. When you do this, the question you'll ask yourself is simple but profound: *"If I keep doing what I'm doing now, how will my life look in 5 years?"* I remember the first time I asked this question of myself. I was drinking by myself at a bar because none of my drinking partners could make it out with me.

I don't remember if I cried then. It's unlikely, but I can tell you that as I'm writing this, that I'm getting a little misty-eyed. That's because I answered the question truthfully. Now, this doesn't mean that I acted upon the realization immediately. It just means that I understood, intellectually, that my behavior was unsustainable.

A note about some things in this last paragraph which may not be obvious, but requires further explanation if you are to get something out of this letter. First, when I say that I *"understood, intellectually"*, this means that I could see the most likely outcome of my behavior. This doesn't mean that I yet had a strong emotional impetus to change. It only means that from that point forward, I could no longer form a rational argument defending my actions. Or to put it another way, I could no longer bullshit myself.

The second point is implied in the first and is more of a general life lesson. Without a strong emotional motivation, it's very difficult to do anything—let alone get sober. Yes, you need a plan and the discipline to execute it, but the plan means nothing without the genuine desire to execute.

For example, no one can force you to go through an intervention or the 12 steps to sobriety, regardless of how badly you need them. On the flip side, once you decide that you want to be sober more than anything, you won't actually need any program or outside interference.

I wanted to be more, but I thought I could balance it with alcohol. I thought I could be a high performer with an excellent life and a heavy drinker. That wasn't in the cards for me. Clearly, there are some people who can get to the top and simultaneously be functioning addicts. This wasn't me, but I desperately wanted it to be. It's probably a good thing that I couldn't be because it would mask the problem I had. I'd always be able to justify things because my life is fine in most areas.

I thought I could be a good friend and maintain an excellent personal reputation while under the influence. This is one of the illusions of competence that alcohol is notorious for creating. Your relationships are important—probably the most important thing to you in the world—so you will get tired of straining them. Fortunately for you, you get tired of straining them before they get tired of supporting you. But it's an unnecessary stress. A stress that, in this lonely moment at the bar, you'll realize is unsustainable. Only intellectually of course, but now you're no longer in denial about it.

You will change because you know that what you are doing isn't working. Without this awareness and understanding, there's nothing you can do about any problem. Even if you don't believe you can change, all that's required at this point is understanding that you must change. This applies to every hardship and addiction. If you don't think it's a problem, you won't even make the effort to fix it.

While the emotional decision to stop drinking will take you some time to make, this realization puts the wheels in motion. Now it's only a matter of time.

There are only two ways to sobriety for people like us: the easy way or the hard way. The easy way is what you do, and what I like to believe most people do. You stop drinking, make some lifestyle changes, and commit to sobriety. It's not a complicated process, but it is one that requires discipline and vigilance. Most importantly, it's a process that you engage in voluntarily.

The hard way is not voluntary. It's becoming incapacitated, incarcerated, or deceased. It's hard to get alcohol in prison and impossible to drink it if you're dead. In these conditions, it's inevitable that you'll get sober, but at the expense of your freedom or life. This isn't a price you want to pay.

So, one way or another, addicts get sober. This is how I know that you'll get sober; and it won't be the hard way. For a short while, you'll feel like you don't have much to live for, so the hard way looks more likely. Then you'll meet a person who sees something in you that makes you want to be better. You'll start a slow process of life improvement because now freedom and living looks more appealing.

Herein lies a great a secret of sobriety and general life improvement. You must believe that your life is worth something. If you don't believe in the worth of your own life, you'll never emotionally commit to solving the intellectual realization that you have a problem with alcohol. I used to always believe that my presence wouldn't be missed and that I'm largely expendable. For the most part, I assumed that people tolerated me rather than desired my presence.

Yes, this makes you prone to drinking for acceptance, but it also makes you numb to self-destructive behavior. You know the risks, but since you don't care about yourself or think that anyone else does, the risks are acceptable to take. It wasn't until I started to believe that I had value to people beyond a source of entertainment or as a drinking partner that I wanted to be more and better.

I'm disclosing a powerful secret. Just because I'm telling it to you doesn't mean that it's guaranteed to pass. I'm here, I've gone through it, and I know who I am because of it. But who are you? You are a person who hasn't had these experiences yet. I'm not just talking to my former self, but to anyone who is having trouble finding sufficient reason to change self-destructive behavior.

When you feel worthwhile, you're more likely to do things which preserve that worth and cease things which erode it. Low self-esteem is the root behind most self-destructive behavior. This is somewhat obvious, but a bigger problem is that low self-esteem can be surprisingly difficult to detect. Once it's detected, there is a simple solution, but it's not easy.

Look around and learn to trust the humans you like and show signs of liking you in return. This solution is carefully chosen, based not only on my own experience but on sorting out all the stories and experiences of others.

We bond with people who like us. There are people who like us for reasons other than just a person to drink with. It may take trial and error to find these people, but they're often hidden in plain sight. They've been your friends for years before you put the quantity of friendships over the quality. These are the people who like you just for you, and for no other reason. You truly can *"be yourself"* around them.

But who are you, really? This is a simplified version, to be expanded upon in another letter, but you are the person whom alcohol keeps dumb and down. You are a person who loves learning and competing. You'd rather spend the evening at a museum or jazz club than perched on a bar stool. You want to learn how the world works and become interesting, but you believe the best way to do this is by drinking. In short, you're misguided.

When you start building the life you want, you'll attract the people into it who make it fulfilling. These will most likely not be the people who were your drinking partners. These will be the people who support you and bring the best out of you. This is where you'll not just learn who you are but love who you are as well.

But first, you must trust. A little self-delusion goes a long way. There's someone in your life who likes you regardless of whether you drink or not. Find this person and spend time with them. If you don't have this person, pour yourself into something that contributes to and changes the world positively. You don't want to spend too much time by yourself because right now, you don't know who you are and are more likely to revert to the behaviors of the person you think that you are—the alcoholic.

Once you believe you are worthwhile, you'll have emotional fuel to make more lasting and effective changes. You will not only know that you are capable of more, but you'll believe it as well. This is everything. This is how I know that you will get sober and I know that anyone who knows their drinking is a problem will get sober. You don't have a choice. One way or the other, you will put the bottle down.

The Three Things You Need to Stop Drinking

I know that you've always questioned alcohol. You can't quite work out the benefit you get from drinking, but it is part of the social scene. The socialization component of alcohol keeps you from feeling like an outcast. So you continue to drink, and with your personality, this always means drinking hard.

Now that I'm sober, I'm careful to never suggest sobriety to anyone. I don't consider this an effective method for getting people to take action. If they're ready, they will reach out to me or someone else. If they aren't, then the only thing that my preaching will do is annoy them. I don't judge people who drink, even if their behavior makes it obvious that they shouldn't. However, when a person asks me about my experience with sobriety, I sing nothing but praise about the decision to get on the wagon.

Getting sober is probably the best decision you'll ever make. It's going to change everything in your life for the better. There is nothing lost when you quit drinking. However, you will get back so much, including things that you didn't even know you had lost.

So, if I believe that sobriety is such a powerful tool, why am I not an outspoken champion for it? Why don't I go around denouncing the evils of alcohol to anyone who will listen? I'm silent on the topic for two reasons.

The first reason is that this type of behavior is obnoxious. It gives off an aura of superiority that everyone finds insufferable. You already struggle with feelings of being outcast, but those are mainly just feelings. Few people are physically ostracized for NOT drinking. Constantly talking about your sobriety and criticizing those who still drink will make your illusions of separation a reality.

The second reason I don't randomly proclaim the benefits of sobriety is why I'm writing to you in this letter. I don't tell people they should give up alcohol because everyone has to make that decision on their own. It can't come from the pressure of society, family or friends. Interventions sometimes work in spite of themselves, but the victory is short-lived. If an alcoholic doesn't want to stop, then they won't stick it out. As the old saying goes, *"He who is convinced against his will, remains of the same opinion still."*

Whether you have a drinking problem or problems while drinking, transitioning to sobriety can be challenging. You need powerful reasons to stay committed to sobriety, otherwise environmental and social pressures will pull you off the wagon.

After comparing my own experiences to the experiences of others, I've figured out the three things you must do that will greatly increase your chances of remaining committed to sobriety. Doing these three things will put the power back in your hands and give you the confidence you need to remain sober.

Admit Your Fears

The first thing you must do is admit that you're afraid. This fear grants you a healthy humility towards the process and ensures that you take it seriously. It doesn't matter what you're specifically afraid of, but you must acknowledge that you ARE afraid.

What are some things that you're possibly afraid of? There have already been tragic events in your past that make you think that you drink too much. These events are never positive, but you can always justify them to yourself. Or worse, other people make excuses for you—even the people you hurt.

The usual excuse for your behavior is *"blame it on the alcohol."* It's such a common mantra that there was even a popular song with this title. Our society conditions us to believe that if the offense was not too egregious, and it was committed under the influence of alcohol, that all is well and will be forgiven.

However, this forgiveness has a finite limit. You'll either do one big thing or several smaller ones, but the patience with your behavior will eventually be exhausted. The people who drank with you will no longer be able to stand you. Your family and friends will abandon you, and you'll have no one to blame but yourself.

There is also the possibility of causing damage to yourself or your surroundings. Every alcoholic I know, including myself, thought it was a good idea to drive a car under the influence. The good news for you is that you will stop drinking before you get a criminal record or harm anyone. However, you must remember that no one outruns the law of large numbers forever.

You can only avoid the legal consequences of breaking the law for so long. Once they catch up to you, your life becomes far more difficult than it needs to be. Consider the ramifications of a DUI, or worse, a vehicular homicide charge. When you're younger, these things don't scare you as much as they should. Eventually, they will. Alcoholic behavior and the actions that accompany it will eventually repel those close to you and put you in grave danger.

There is another fear that you must acknowledge. That is the fear of change and being different. You're afraid that if you stop drinking, you'll miss out on the social experience. Instead of worrying that people will leave you behind for your bad behavior, you're afraid that they will desert you for your good behavior instead.

The fear of being alone has kept you drinking for many more years than you wanted it to. Alcohol was never that enjoyable to you, but the socialization rituals surrounding it made it so. At the very least, it was preferable to being alone.

In your mind, sobriety means giving up a large part of this social life. This is terrifying. You may not think about this constantly, but it's in the back of every drinker's mind. It's one of the things that all recovering alcoholics warn you about.

Your new habits almost necessitate forming new friends. This must be done, if for any other reason than we are a product of our environment. I was lucky because my closest friends didn't abandon me, but many people are afraid of losing the life they once knew.

There is no easy remedy for your fear of change. The only thing you can do is recognize that a new lifestyle scares you, and make the change anyway. The same thing goes for your fears of what will happen if you keep drinking. It is only by recognizing these fears that you can do anything about them.

Admitting that you have a problem is the first step in recovery, but part of that is realizing that you're afraid. You're afraid of what happens if you keep drinking. You're afraid of what happens when you stop. This is the part of the problem that you must accept before you can work on finding a solution.

A Reason Why

Strong fears will keep you away from self-destructive behavior while a powerful motivation pulls you towards the goal. It's not enough to be afraid of what can go wrong. It's not enough to simply want to stop. You also need a positive and powerful reason to stay on the path of sobriety.

If you're only afraid of what can go wrong, how does this make you any different than your previous self? Everyone is afraid of what can go wrong. Part of being human is that we're afraid of the negative consequences that accompany mistakes. Especially the big mistakes that cost us our relationships or freedom.

One way alcoholics try to mitigate this fear is through a type of insurance or self-imposed barrier against their worst tendencies. We try to drink only a few beers, or not text people while under the influence, or leave our keys with someone so they we don't get behind the wheel. These approaches never work.

They never work because we have free will. If you want your keys back, you'll fight to get your keys back. You're going to text that person the moment you get a chance to because alcohol has destroyed your ability to make rational judgments. After a few drinks, the path to bad decisions becomes even more alluring. Alcohol fueled irrational self-confidence and diminished self-control easily topples soberly erected barriers after only a few drinks.

We try to ensure ourselves against our worst selves, but we ultimately fail. We're a ticking time bomb, and with each passing hour and a sip of alcohol, the timer moves closer to zero. When one is operating on fear alone, the focus is on avoiding the consequences rather than maximizing the benefits.

I don't know if many other drinkers go through this phase, but there was a period where I knew that I was a danger to myself and others while drinking. I wasn't motivated to quit, but I was afraid of how bad things could get if I drank too much. The irony of this approach is that I often tried to drink away this fear so that I could socialize more easily, and I arrogantly (and wrongly) believed that I was in control.

A healthy fear of the consequences is important, but using them alone to curb your alcoholic tendencies has another serious drawback. We tend to gauge how we should behave by our environment. By this metric, it's easy to justify drinking to excess because so many other people are doing it.

There were several instances when you didn't want to drink heavy, but everyone in your social circle did. Maybe they were fine, but you still had your demons to battle. This is not to excuse or justify your weakness, but many of us severely underestimate the power of groupthink and peer pressure—especially when this is combined with the desire for approval. When the inner battle starts, your best intentions will always lose to your desire to fit in.

Fear is powerful, but fear alone is inadequate. You also need a reason that will keep you committed to your goal of sobriety. This reason, whatever it is, needs to be explicitly positive. At the very least, it cannot be one that is purely motivated by the desire to avoid the worst things in life.

When you decide to get sober, you'll stand at an important crossroads: You can continue down the dark road you've been going down. You know where it's going. You don't know when it ends, but you know that it will, and you know that it's not where you want to be.

Or...

You can take another route. You can start to seriously pursue your goals and invest in the type of life that you want. For me, I decided that I could make my new relationship work, get my physics degree, pursue my professional boxing career, and seriously focus on writing some books.

These are the things I always wanted, but I couldn't attain until I give up the old me and his old habits. I realized that I couldn't have what I wanted if I spent all my time and energy drinking. This made the decision easier.

There is another benefit of having a goal: It helps you navigate the fear of change. It's one thing to simply give up an old habit. If it's all you've known, and you give it up out of fear, your desire for familiarity will cause you to relapse. However, if you are working towards something new and better, you're more likely to stick to it. These last two points lead nicely into the last thing you need to stop drinking.

A New Habit

No matter why you do it, drinking is a habit. You're addicted to the ritual and the associated feelings. You associate it with good times, socialization, and validation. Drinking is also your automatic response to an intense emotional stimulus. Before we go further, the latter habitual response requires explanation.

Most of us drink for one of the big C's: catharsis, celebration or coping. When we're stressed or need to blow off steam, we drink to relax. When something good happens, we drink to celebrate. When something tragic happens, we drink to numb the emotional impact. Alcohol is the automatic response to our emotional state, regardless of its type or intensity.

By extension, this means that the tendency to drink is ingrained in most societies. If you grew up in a community where this is the norm, then it's already an expectation that you'll drink in response to nearly every situation imaginable.

Our awareness of alcohol starts when we are children. We see beer at every social function. By the time we're old enough to drink, we already believe that social events aren't entertaining or mature if they don't have alcohol, and nowhere is this more apparent than in college.

Here it's expected that you'll drink hard on the weekends but keep it (somewhat) under control during the week. There's even a pregame ritual where you drink before you go out to drink even more with your friends. With so much activity focused on drinking, it is ensured that any good times you have will be inextricably linked to alcohol.

This continues well into adulthood. Once you reach your mid-twenties, everyone meets and socializes around a happy hour function. Alcohol is the centerpiece and keystone of your social life. Without it, you feel as if your connection to humanity would disintegrate.

If you're serious about sobriety, you must replace your rituals, reasons, and habits with ones that are conducive to your goal. The habits don't need to be complicated. They only need to be effective. You can't just stop drinking. That's a recipe for disaster. You must fill your new sober time with something constructive and meaningful.

One of my worst habits was the need to always have a drink in my hand. I hated feeling empty-handed. Not only did I need a cup or bottle in my hand, but it needed to have some weight, so I always kept it full. Even sober, I generally feel uneasy with an empty cup or glass in my vicinity, whether it be in my hand or sitting down.

Not having something in my hand would have been a disaster. This would have removed the habit without replacing it with something constructive. First, I tried water but it was too easy to finish and lacked flavor. So, I started to drink coffee instead. I eventually discovered a line of non-alcoholic beers and so I not only replaced the weight, but I also found a tasty beverage that let me feel like I fit in.

I used to drink to celebrate. Once I got sober, I knew that I needed a new habit for celebrating the good times in my life. Instead of heading to the bar or picking up a bottle on the way home, I celebrate by having dinner with my girlfriend. This is way more constructive than drinking and it allows me to form non-alcohol related associations to positive events in my life.

When I was stressed, I used to drink. Once I decided that would no longer be an option, I had to find something new to handle my stress. I began to write. Now when something is troubling me, and I need to think, I start jotting down my thoughts. This is more constructive and healthier than drinking my distress away. It also has the added benefit of developing material for me to share on my blog so others can learn from my experiences and realizations.

These habits are only suggestions. They're what work for me. You can do whatever it takes to replace your reasons for and habits associated with drinking. Every drinking habit is slightly different, but the general suggestion is the same. Find a beneficial and constructive alternative to replace the moments when you would drink to celebrate, cope, or engage in catharsis.

Summary

You need three things to stop drinking. You need to acknowledge that you're afraid. If you don't do this, you aren't giving sobriety its proper respect. Fear demonstrates your respect. It's a challenge, but acknowledging your worries gives you the best chance of making a change.

You need a goal. This is the thing that drives you to stop drinking. There must be something you want that your drinking is keeping you from attaining. If you don't have a compelling reason driving you to stop drinking, then it's not likely that you'll stick to it.

Lastly, you need to form new habits and rituals to replace your old ones. Without a new habit to take the place of the old one, then the vacuum left behind may be filled with something even more destructive.

Fear keeps you from regressing, goals give you the drive to move forward, and new habits make it easy for all the effort to last.

Drunk Thoughts, Sober Decisions

Being an alcoholic is more than just a dependency on alcohol. Alcoholism is also greater than an inability to limit your consumption and control your actions while under its influence. By themselves, these actions are stupid and dangerous, yet they do not signify any chronic dysfunction.

However, this doesn't mean that you are not held accountable for your actions while under the influence. You absolutely are. After all, no one gets a DUI for just thinking about downing a fifth of Jack Daniels before getting behind the wheel. Once you do a thing, there are consequences, many of which persist regardless of how long it's been since your last drink.

Someone once told me that an alcoholic is always either drunk or thinking about getting drunk. I believe this is true but requires further explanation. For a while, I disagreed with the statement. Why? Well, when I drank, I never felt anxious or withdrawn from booze. I wasn't consciously thinking about getting drunk. I clearly thought this was either false information or I didn't have an alcohol problem.

Upon evaluating myself, I realized that it's because I didn't have to. I'm an extroverted, action-oriented person who doesn't like to spend more time than necessary in his head. As a result, I never thought about drinking. Instead, I just made plans to drink.

Since I knew all the happy the local hour drink specials, party hosts, and the work schedules of all my friends, I never had to think about consuming alcohol. If none of my friends were available, I had no problem finding people to drink with. My entire social life was centered around the consumption of alcohol. If a person or an event didn't offer me a way to drink, I didn't want anything to do with it.

In effect, I planned my entire life around drinking. I never noticed thinking about alcohol because I didn't have to. Subconscious thoughts and immediate desires of getting drunk influenced my sober decisions to the point where I didn't notice I had a telltale sign of alcoholism.

Doing The Math

You're a person who values your time, therefore, efficiency is important to you. This means that if you want to get the most out of drinking, you need to plan, calculate, and anticipate. Now that I'm sober, I call this *"doing the math"*.

When you start to mathematically calculate your drinking, you're in trouble. Sometimes it's a matter of working out how much money you can afford to spend. Other times, it's figuring how much alcohol you need to consume to remain drunk for the remainder of the night.

The planning itself isn't the problem; in fact, some might argue that planning your drinking is responsible. However, the problem arises when you start structuring important events in your life to accommodate your drinking. Cautiousness and prudence are one thing; avoiding situations which do not permit drinking is another matter altogether. You don't need to think about drinking, because the plan to do so is already in place.

This has an immense effect on your personal life. For instance, the availability of alcohol determines who you visit during holidays and which friends you spend time with. Although people regularly decide how to divide their time amongst personal connections, your problem is that the decision is purely influenced by your ability to consume alcohol.

In the beginning, no one notices this; after all, everyone drinks. In our teens and early twenties, the alcohol supply determines which parties we attend. Unfortunately, this factor alone begins to determine which social and family functions you attend and how much time you spend at them; the length being determined by how long the alcohol is available. If you HAVE to attend a *"dry"* function you manage to figure out ways to sneak in one of your trusty flasks.

That's when it hits you; it's not an 'aha' moment, however, it does prompt careful consideration. If alcohol wasn't involved, would you still plan to see these people? If the answer is no, then your issue extends beyond the scope of this section. However, if the answer is yes, then you have a dependency on alcohol.

This realization does not elicit an admission of alcoholism. However, it is one of the first times you realize that you make plans based on the possibility of being able to get drunk.

You were going to see many of these people anyway; you like them, enjoy their company, and they bring value to your life. However, if they didn't have alcohol, you would consider not seeing them. At the very least, would you consider not seeing them if you didn't bring your own supply of alcohol?

Beyond interactions with various people, there are certain activities which you enjoy; writing and boxing are some of your favorite pastimes. It's easy to justify drinking and writing. There is a romantic notion of writers scribing the night away while sipping a glass of chardonnay. For many aspiring writers, the two activities go together like bacon and eggs. Since you manage to get a lot of writing done while drinking, you never question the effects of this combination.

As time progresses, your physical health suffers because you began to plan your workouts around drinking. Going to the bar after the gym becomes more important than relaxation and recovery. Sometimes, you even go to the gym after having a few drinks. I didn't go straight to the bar from the gym. Instead, I tried to do the math. However, I was usually wrong and it was obvious.

We mainly focus on our actions while under the influence, but this is only part of the issue. A larger problem is the lifestyle choices which are made to facilitate constant alcohol consumption. To demonstrate this, ask yourself the following simple question:

If I had to choose between drinking and another activity, which would I select?

When alcohol takes precedence over your needs, activities, and loved ones, you have a problem. Even if you chose the other activities, but only by a narrow margin, you need to rethink your relationship with alcohol.

You may make your decisions while sober, but you are making them with a drunken mindset.

An Alcohol Problem or Problems On Alcohol

When I decided to stop drinking, I went to my first Alcoholics Anonymous (AA) meeting. I didn't return to another meeting for 4 years, but I stayed sober and learned something very important.

There are two types of people who shouldn't drink: those who have an alcohol problem and those who have problems while under the influence of alcohol. Although individuals in both categories are alcoholics, the heavy drinkers of the first type are the ones who get the most attention.

An Alcohol Problem

An individual with an alcohol problem is what typically comes to mind when we think of an alcoholic. These are the people who drink so much and so frequently that only an ungodly amount of liquor makes them inebriated. Moreover, they can't go too long between drinks because many of them experience withdrawal symptoms. Their compulsion for drinking is impossible for most people to understand. It is truly an addiction.

Those who suffer from an alcohol problem will know they have a problem, as will everyone around them. Alcohol rules their lives. They effectively cannot survive without consuming alcohol. For whatever reason, they cannot merely have one drink. These are the types of people I most encountered at the AA meetings. There are mixed opinions regarding AA. Some people don't like the ideology of AA and believe that it's ineffective. Others give the organization sole credit for their double-digit years of sobriety.

Regardless of one's personal perspective, there is a crucial component of AA which cannot be refuted: AA clearly identifies the culprit.

The first step of the AA program is *"We admitted we were powerless over alcohol and that our lives had become unmanageable."* Admitting the existence of a problem comes first and for good reason: a problem cannot be dealt with unless it is first acknowledged. If you don't know what your problem is, then there's nothing you can do to fix it.

People who suffer from alcohol problems are powerless against the substance. They must avoid alcohol at all costs. This can be accomplished in various ways, ranging from sheer willpower to leaning on a support system to even turning to religion. How they keep their distance isn't important. All that matters is they stay away from alcohol because failure to do so will destroy all aspects of their lives.

I heard several stories in AA from people who were on their last chance. I listened to stories of people who got multiple DUIs and mandatory AA sessions were a condition of prison release. A woman broke into tears as she shared her story about losing her children to protective services due to alcohol-related incidents. As I digested different stories about the various tumultuous paths that brought different people to the church basement where the meeting was held, I had two major thoughts.

First, I thought about the amount of luck I must have. I was lucky that my relationship with alcohol didn't lead to a jail term or a tragedy. There were many situations where the police would have been well within their rights to take me to jail, but they didn't—and those are just the times I actually got caught while driving under the influence of alcohol. Listening to the stories of other people's misfortune made me grateful that I was getting things together before it was too late.

My second thought was that I was a different type of alcoholic. In retrospect, it seems arrogant to think this. While I understood that my relationship with alcohol was not superior in comparison to the other AA attendees, I also realized that I had a different problem: I did not have an alcohol dependency problem; I could abstain from drinking without a problem. My problems happened when I drank. I had problems while under the influence of alcohol.

Problems On Alcohol

The difference between the two is a matter of type, not degree. I used to say that alcohol caused or exacerbated 95% percent of my problems. I didn't need to drink, but whenever I did, it unleashed the worst parts of me. For instance, I was never a fighter because violence isn't part of my personality. However, I would lose all emotional control and discipline after drinking.

I also encountered some people at AA who only had problems while drinking alcohol. Like me, these individuals did not have a dependency on alcohol, their issues only arrived after consumption. Though we have no problem staying away from alcohol, having only one drink is never possible. For people like us, it's always all-or-nothing. Our hesitation to admit the existence of a problem is because this segment of the problem is overlooked. In fact, being this type of alcoholic is often revered and celebrated amongst our friends.

The ability to drink to extremes is treated as a badge of honor throughout one's early twenties. Those who can drink hard, heavy, and often are treated like local celebrities and revered as gods the next morning. Conversely, those who can't *"hold their liquor"* are ridiculed for their inability to keep pace with the collective self-destruction of their peers. This social ritual is responsible for more alcoholics than the alcohol companies themselves.

If there's anything you become addicted to, it's the ritual and celebration of this lifestyle. This eventually leads to the inability to distinguish between good feelings resulting from intoxication and the good feelings resulting from adoration. This begins a vicious cycle: you drink to feel like you belong, and you only feel like you belong when you drink.

This hedonistic path of self-destruction was compounded by my personality of extremes. The desire to feel important, coupled with the inability to be alone fuels many nights where you know you should stop drinking, but my fear of seclusion keeps you going well past your limits. One of your biggest problems with alcohol is that it's temporary relief to a permanent problem. The cost of the solution often exceeds its value.

Your failure to recognize your alcoholism is also related to your surroundings and peers. Since everyone around you is drinking heavily, this behavior is considered normal. After all, you're just a young person drinking alcohol at a level deemed acceptable by much of society. However, your combination of personality traits and specific issues make you susceptible to the addictive properties of alcohol. The environment that you consider normal is not normal. The environment which many people function in (or appear to, anyhow) is not an environment in which you will survive.

To this day, I don't know the amount of time it takes for a person to discover their issues with alcohol. If my situation is any indication, many people never realize they're using alcohol as an addictive band-aid or an escape mechanism. In college, I lived on a floor with an 18-year-old kid who refilled his liquor fridge every 3 days. He had to refill it so frequently because he started and ended each day with a drink. Eventually, he had to leave the university because his work was suffering. This type of drinking problem is easy to identify because it mirrors the common thoughts and perceptions of alcoholism. However, what about the rest of us?

In other cases, the problems are harder to catch and they take longer to manifest since we're only getting hammered on the weekends. Those of us who have a problem with alcohol fit in for a long time. We drink hard yet nothing seems out of the ordinary because everyone that age feels like they're supposed to drink hard. Popular opinion and societal trends would say I didn't have a drinking problem, however, history has shown us that what is popular is rarely what is correct.

People who become violent, overly emotional, or inappropriately sexual only under the influence of alcohol have a problem with the substance. The same principle applies to individuals who make stupid and dangerous decisions only when they've been drinking. The individuals in these categories have problems while under the influence of alcohol. They have the same problem that I do.

This should not be surprising. Alcohol is designed to make you act without thought or reservation. While this doesn't spell disaster for everyone, the actions you take while intoxicated are a function of probability: the drunker you become, the greater your chances are to do something that permanently alters your life—and not usually for the best. You can be fine 90% of the time, and the remaining 10% can be enough to ruin your life, friendships, and self-respect.

Since everyone views their mishaps as the cost of doing business, catching on to the problem of this type of alcoholic can take quite some time. Often, your drinking antics are readily forgiven; the younger you are, the more you can hide behind the excuse of being drunk. However, as you get older, your drinking problem will become more obvious and you will also notice more people drifting away from you.

An alcohol problem is easy to identify because the frequency of the person's drinking is apparent. The social stigma associated with this alcoholic's manner of drinking also makes the problem quicker to notice. If you have an alcohol problem, you'll know early on if you're an alcoholic.

People who have problems while under the influence go unnoticed because they look like everyone else. While these problems initially appear as the familiar casualties of young adult drinking, they eventually become larger and beyond management.

In the beginning, these people look like typical 20-something-year-olds who like to party. It eventually becomes clear that some of us get drunk to escape while the rest of us are in pursuit of what we feel is missing from our lives. Their motivations may initially be benign, but they morph into a more sinister element which lurks beneath the surface. Soon, their true nature becomes obvious to everyone around them.

I am the alcoholic who has problems while drinking. I'm fortunate to realize this before doing irreparable damage to the most sacred parts of my life. Regardless of whether you have a drinking problem or problems while drinking, sobriety is a choice. You will make it. Even though you don't know it yet, this decision will change your life.

A Product Of Your Environment

Personalities, habits, and tendencies are not formed in a vacuum. Who you are, how you respond, and what you think is all influenced by your environment. While your personality is innate and mostly genetic, the expression of it depends on what you've been exposed to. Furthermore, different environments give different feedback, reinforcing or deterring certain behaviors. Understanding this feedback mechanism is crucial for dealing with your drinking.

Imagine that your personality tends towards aggressive and risk-taking behaviors. If you participate in combat sports from an early age, you quickly learn that there is negative feedback for uncontrolled aggression and unnecessary risk (losing); and there is positive feedback for controlled aggression and calculated risk (winning). As you succeed, you develop the ability to control your personality and mitigate the worst parts of it. This, in turn, earns you respect and admiration, which makes it less likely you'll be put in situations to indulge your worst tendencies.

In boxing, we learn that it's easier to execute when we remain calm after sustaining damage. We learn how to suffer embarrassment without embarrassing ourselves. There is a culture of respect that permeates the boxing gym, and that respect is enforced by violent men who are also in control of their worst tendencies?.

To succeed, self-control is a must. If you lose it in the ring, you lose. If you lose it outside of the ring, you risk extrication. In this way, you learn to keep the worst expressions of yourself in check, and this attitude permeates everything that you do.

Things may turn out differently if you grow up in an environment lacking discipline and order. Your aggressive tendencies will never be properly checked and balanced. Your environment will not only fail to channel these traits into something more constructive, but it will disincentivize and discourage you from getting control of yourself.

Social environments are built by the personalities who regularly interact with them. If you get along with a new group of people, it's because the dynamic of the group is a natural fit for your personality. Or, at the very least, you can mold your personality in such a way that it fits the group. For better or worse, most of us don't regularly interact with people who have different ideas and values. Instead, we find people who act and think like us to spend most of our time around.

This isn't good or bad. It's merely a function of human interaction. We not only gravitate towards people who are like us, but we are influenced by their thoughts and characteristics. If you start spending time with a group of people because you have one thing in common, it's likely that you're going to pick up some of their other interests. They're also going to pick up some of yours. Your personality and interests pull you towards a certain environment, and the environment reinforces the personality and interests that initially drew you to the environment.

Although drinking is something you have in common with many of your friends, it wasn't always this way. We shared something benign before we ever shared a bottle. We were classmates, coworkers, or maybe lifelong friends. Then alcohol was introduced and suddenly, our microcosm of personal commonality was sucked into the macrocosm of societal alcohol use. Now every social event must involve alcohol, or else it's viewed as childish or *"lame"*.

By itself, this isn't a problem. The problem occurs when you decide that you no longer wish to drink. You're able to stop drinking for a few days, and then you realize that you are alone. Your environment was defined by alcohol and now that you aren't drinking, you feel an invisible pressure from this environment to go back to what you've come to know. Even if no one directly pressures you to take a drink, being in the old environment makes it difficult to abolish old habits. This is the inevitable result of trying to exist in an old environment while trying to build new behaviors.

If you stay with sobriety long enough, something powerful will happen. It will become more difficult to take a drink than it is to not. This is what happens after you've been sober for some time. Your perspective of the world without alcohol becomes strong because of the time you invested in your sobriety. You've spent significant time not drinking and as a result, you know how to confidently live without it.

In the beginning, the social pressure, and soft ostracization that accompanies sobriety makes you realize that your inability to stay sober mainly comes from a lack of confidence in yourself and your decisions. This pressure is just an illusion. There are many people who resist the siren's call of alcohol.

Why You Give In

Initially, your sobriety habit is not strong enough to carry you through the valley of temptation. Dieters decrease their chances of success if they're around the foods they want to cut back on. Alcoholics jeopardize their recovery by spending time around alcohol. Temptation is discipline's greatest opponent and biggest obstacle. Until healthy eating is fortified as a physical, mental, and emotional habit, your best chance for success is completely removing the foods from your vicinity.

Even if you understand the destructiveness of eating certain foods, the temptation to indulge exists during the early stages of your diet because old emotions conflict with your new rationality. Intellectually, you know that your drinking prevents you from making progress. However, you still feel the desire to drink when around alcohol because you haven't viscerally accepted this yet. The pressure you feel is your environment attempting to reinforce your old habits.

Your environment is more powerful than your new habits. Your environment is more powerful than your new values. Your environment dictates who you'll become if you don't strongly believe in who you currently are. When you try to change a habit that your environment reinforces, your environment will pressure you to stay exactly as you are.

A big reason people fail to get sober is that their new habit is weak and their old environment is strong. All new sober ideas, feelings, and habits are frail in comparison. We protect new life from the world because it is not yet strong enough to walk on its own. We develop new ideas until they're strong enough to stand on their own against more established motifs and models. We do this because there is no way for something new to compete against something more developed.

Your drinking habit is refined enough to walk on its own and stand against anything that challenges it. Your sobriety is a new habit, without much time or experience behind it. In comparison, it is barely crawling. When the old drinking environment clashes with your sober intentions, you will be drawn back into drinking every time. The only way to win this battle is to not fight it in the first place.

Change Your Environment, Change Your Life

One way or the other, you'll have to change your environment. Either the people and places you were once affiliated with will exile you, or you'll exile them. Once you're serious about getting sober, you'll realize that it's impossible to simultaneously live in the old and new world.

Sobriety is just a habit. If excessive drinking can be a habit, then so can excessive restraint. Like all habits, it requires effort at the beginning but then it eventually goes on autopilot. This gross simplification may not be entirely accurate, but it does provide a useful framework for us to form a powerful strategy for conquering our drinking.

If you view your sobriety as a habit, you can strengthen it by repetition. We're no longer trying to break the habit of drinking. Rather, we're trying to build the habit of sobriety. Not only does this make it easier for you to stop drinking, but it also illustrates the importance of your environment.

We know that an environment filled with the thing you're trying to avoid makes it difficult to remain disciplined. Humans seek the path of least resistance with the greatest reward. Giving in to your habit is following the path of least resistance. Part of what makes it a habit is that you don't think about doing it. You're just responding to your environmental stimuli.

This is why you must change your environment if you want to change your life. Your old environment—the environment you used to drink in—is associated with intoxication. Being there, or any place like it will make you feel like you must take a drink—even if you've committed to sobriety.

Initially, I underestimated the power of this principle. There were many times I wanted to quit drinking, but after a few moments in a familiar environment with familiar habits, I was drinking. Habits are so powerful that they often make us act opposite of our best interests and desires. The friction of cognitive dissonance can wear down even the most desperate commitment to change your life.

You are a product of your environment, and your environment reinforces who are. When you change your habits, you are fundamentally changing who you are. You are replacing a destructive behavior with a more constructive one. The more your environment rewards the old behavior, the more it is reinforced, and its antithesis is discouraged.

Until you've strengthened the habit, you will remain susceptible to influences from your surroundings. While I hesitate to say that it's impossible, getting sober while spending time around people and places where drinking is the norm is very difficult. Either you'll feel uncomfortable in the old environment or the old environment will feel uncomfortable with you in it. You'll remove yourself, or it will remove you from it.

Dealing With The Separation

The following advice may be difficult to follow, but it will make a tremendous difference. While you're getting sober, stay away from everything you've known in relation to drinking. Keep your distance from anyone, anything or any place that you drank around. Not indefinitely, but at least for the period while you are adjusting and developing your sobriety habit.

Within the old environment are the friends you regularly drank with. You'll have to stop seeing them for a while as well. You must disinvite yourself from any group setting where alcohol is present. These environments may not make you start drinking immediately, but they will plant seeds of doubt in your mind and make you question your commitment to sobriety.

Your friends aren't going to scold you for your heavy drinking and your intoxicated antics. It's not because they don't care about you, but very often it's because they don't see it as a problem. Sure, they may not like you when you're drunk, but they must normalize their drinking as well. This means that your friends, though they care for you the most, are the people least likely to give you honest feedback about your drinking.

The first piece of honest feedback I got about my drinking and habits came from people who, despite masquerading as my friends, didn't like me. Eventually, they became open with their hostilities and we went our separate ways. Although I considered them enemies for a long time, they are the people who got me to first consider that I had a problem. Though we no longer communicate, I am grateful for their actions.

Your enemies are far more honest with you than your friends will ever be. Your friends have something to lose. They not only risk being forced to examine themselves in a critical light, but they also risk turning you into an enemy. Your enemies don't care what you think, and they already dislike you. They aren't necessarily incentivized towards honesty, as they gain nothing from lying to you about your character flaws.

When you're in your old environment with your old friends, you'll see everyone having a great time and you'll feel left out. You'll start wonder what the big deal about your drinking ever was. Your sobriety will end as quickly as it began. I've experienced this and seen it play often enough to know the validity of this prediction.

You are a product of your environment, and your environment reinforces who you are. The old you is a drinker. The new you is sober. Until you've built up confidence in the new you, the old environment will take you back to the old you. Make this change, stick to it, and the future is yours.

How to Have Fun And Socialize Sober

In modern civilization, people build their entire social lives around drinking. It's no surprise that most people don't know how to socialize alcohol-free and have fun sober. Drinking and socializing are an inseparable pair in our society. Most people have no idea how to have fun without alcohol. If you're thinking of trying sobriety, you're probably worried that you'll be bored to death or become a social outcast. For most drinkers, socializing sober is synonymous with extreme boredom and isolation.

Humans are naturally social creatures. One of the scariest things about getting sober is the fear of having solitary confinement inflicted on your social life. Perhaps you're already sober and you haven't figured out how to have a social life as fulfilling as the one from your drinking days. Maybe you have no plans to stop drinking, but you feel trapped by your inability to socialize without alcohol.

It doesn't matter what your situation is. The only thing that matters is your desire to relearn the lost art of socializing without alcohol and having fun sober. I won't give you a list of sober activities to do for fun. More than likely, you and I will not like the same things.

Old Drinking Environment vs The New Sober You

The most important thing for you to realize your inability to socialize without alcohol is that it's all in your head. Most people—especially drunk people—don't care how much you drink. You only think they do because everyone is terrible at socializing, regardless of their intoxication levels.

The typical interaction goes like this:

Drinking friend: What are you having to drink? The first round's on me

You: Nah. I'm good.

Drinking friend: WHAT! C'mon, why aren't you drinking?

Now you feel like you need to explain why you aren't drinking. When you can't come up with an explanation you feel confident enough to stick by, you cave into peer pressure. Rather than staying committed to your goal, you fail to remain sober.

I know you really wanted to try to not drink tonight.
I know that you're tired of wasting every weekend hungover.

None of these things matter because, despite your best intentions, you have no idea how to handle this situation. You feel weak or failing to remain committed to not drinking. To the rest of the world, you look just like another person who gave into the slightest force of peer pressure.

The reality is that the person who does the pressuring is weak and the friend who gives in is merely responding to familiar environmental cues which triggered an old habit.

The person who puts the pressure on you to drink is always insecure. I know this from playing both sides of the field; being both the sober friend and the one who tries to get the other friend to drink. Understanding this dynamic allows you to grasp why you feel like you need alcohol to socialize and have fun.

The problem is that your environment is full of people who support each other's decision to drink. Even if only one of them directly confronts you about not drinking, they have the power in numbers. You're trying to start a new action in an old environment, where the numbers are not on your side and—for the moment—you don't know any other way to fit in. When you understand this and how it works, you see why most people fail to socialize sober—especially if they're around people who drink.

Beating The Old Drinking Environment Is The Secret

Understanding the relationship between your old drinking environment and yourself provides valuable insights. You're a product of your environment, and your actions reinforce the strength of your environment. In the battle between the new you and your old environment, there are only two ways to win: changing your environment or building yourself up. Both methods of victory support one another.

Changing your environment helps build a new you. The discomfort and anxiety you feel are just the weaknesses of your new habits facing pressure from your old environment. A new you will allow you to feel comfortable in any environment. This environment exists in your mind more than any place else. The secret to having fun and socializing sober is building a new environment in your mind that supports your sobriety. This is first accomplished by finding a place that allows you to develop the confidence to be sober and have fun.

What Do You Like to Do For Fun?

The usual advice given for socializing without alcohol is to not spend time in bars. While this is generally good advice, it has a glaring flaw—just avoiding bars will not be enough, you can obtain alcohol almost anywhere. In fact, alcohol is so intertwined with our society that there are almost no social events where it's impossible to get a drink.

Sure, it's a bad idea to get blackout drunk at the opera or the museum, but you can easily bring in drinks, sneak in a drink or in many cases, purchase it there. If you're bored or not engaged, you'll figure out a way to drink OR you'll hate being sober so much that you'll start to think that the idea of sober socialization is a scam.

You already know the sober things you like to do for fun. Everyone has something that they enjoy without the need for alcohol. Even the most hardcore partying frat brother has some activity that he doesn't do for shots.

Ask yourself: What is it about these activities that I enjoy?

How do you feel when you do these activities afterward? You could do many other things. Why do this thing in particular? Especially sober. Once you have the answers to these questions, the next question is this:

What do I get out of drinking with people that I don't get from spending time sober with them?

I drank because I wanted to feel connected and fit in. I didn't think I was interesting or cool enough for people to desire my company solely on the merits of my personality. Drinking made me feel like I had a valuable place in a group.

I also realized I drank to pass the time and entertain myself. I couldn't stand the mind-numbing nature of many activities that revolve around drinking. While I'm not a guy who's stuck in his head, I'm happier when I'm learning rather than doing nothing. I always prefer to connect and learn about people rather than form a superficial connection while heavily intoxicated.

To kill that part of me, I drank hard. It soon became the only way I knew how to interact with people because it was a habit built by me, enforced by my environment, and relied on by my mind. It was easy to see that I enjoyed environments where I got mental stimulation or connected with people—preferably, some combination of both. I started spending more time with my friends individually over coffee, rather than in group settings at the bar.

How Less Time Out Taught Me How to Be Social Without Alcohol

By spending more time socializing and enjoying my life on my own terms, I accomplished two different but very important things:

1) I created a habit of being around people without alcohol
2) I created both an external environment and internal space that supported my choice

A big reason you can't socialize without alcohol is that you simply don't know how to. Children do it all the time, but many adults forget how this works. Even if you aren't an alcoholic, there's a good chance you feel uneasy without a drink in your hand at a social function.

You try to have fun sober, but the self-induced pressure makes it very easy to drink—even if you sincerely don't want to. If you learn how to get the feeling you want without the aid of alcohol, you're much better able to socialize sober—even if you're around people who are drinking.

Your confidence will stem from the environment you've developed separately from the drinking environment. This environment has both a physical location and a mental point of origin. Rather than use my old drinking environment to measure my behavior, I measured my mental state against places where I learned to comfortably enjoy myself without alcohol.

Once you can enjoy one part of your life without drinking, you can apply this knowledge to other areas. Whether you want to quit drinking entirely or you only want to take a brief hiatus, this is a powerful technique. However, there is one side effect...

When Drinking Is No Longer Exciting

The better you get at not taking a drink, the less appealing drinking becomes. The less appealing drinking becomes, the less time you'll want to spend around drunk people. You're now the master of the environment that once enslaved you. With this mastery comes boredom.

Once you no longer feel the pressure to drink, you can't help but notice something: almost everyone else is trapped by their inability to socialize and have fun without alcohol. What you do with this information is unique to your purpose and position in life. I occasionally go into a bar, but it's always to eat food. In almost 5 years of sobriety (as of this writing) I can't recall the last time I was just out hanging with people who were doing nothing but drinking.

Some of you will exercise your newly found freedom and still try to socialize with people while they're drinking, but what you will soon learn is that these people—at least while they're drinking—are living in a different world. You now have the ability to come and go as you please. They do not have the luxury.

Ultimately, you learn to cherish what's important to you. Whether it be the connection to people or the location, you regain the ability to enjoy life without diluting it with alcohol.

Connection With The Real You

Reclaiming your identity is a major part of recovery. Depending on how long you've had an alcohol dependency, it may be appropriate to say that you're *"finding"* your identity than *"recovering"* it. Whether the process is one of discovery or rediscovery, the problem is the same: alcohol was part of your identity. Now it is not and you feel lost.

This is the reason is why so many people struggle to socialize without alcohol. Who you socialize with and how you do it is heavily dependent on your personal identity; it would be ridiculous if there wasn't a period of adjustment once you stop drinking. Whether you explicitly ask the question or merely stare at the wall instead of going out with your friends, you'll spend a lot of time wondering "WHO AM I?"

This is not an existential or rhetorical question asked in a moment of crisis. It is an inquiry about your true nature, what matters, and how you want to relate to the world. This question sparks the process of rebuilding, recovering, or reclaiming your identity.

Throughout your drinking, you likely consider alcohol to be an integral part of your personality. You see yourself as a drinker and do things that drinkers do. This is who you are at that time.

However, people who experience normal, healthy relationships with alcohol will consider the preceding context as strange. Long before I entertained the idea that I might have an issue with alcohol, I remember that a woman I dated noted alcohol's involvement in all of my social activities. At the time, I chalked the involvement of alcohol up to the life of a normal 20-something-year-old. Moreover, I thought she was weird for NOT drinking so much.

I don't think any of my close friends shared my same issues with alcohol. However, I do believe that virtually everyone could benefit from reducing their drinking. Nevertheless, I wouldn't fully appreciate the power of this observation until I permanently stopped drinking. Ending a bad habit is like ending a bad relationship: you must fill the void with something positive. If you don't, it's only a matter of time before you return to the familiar destructive entity.

At the root of an alcohol problem is an identity problem. We start drinking because we don't yet know our place in the world and alcohol exaggerates the feelings of belonging and acceptance.

Drinking to build an identity should not be confused with drinking to fit in. *"Fitting in"* is measured externally, while an *"identity"* is measured internally. Invitations to parties and hanging out with popular people is what makes us feel like we're fitting in. This feeling is quite powerful and drives people to do many foolish things. However, feelings of being a social outcast can never be soothed by external approval.

Even if I was invited to hang out with any group of people, I still would have felt the need to drink. Although living up to their expectations played a part, none of the people explicitly told me that I had to drink. These were expectations that I set for myself because I didn't think I was good enough. Since I didn't like myself, I drank to meet an external expectation that wasn't even there.

It was an illusion I desperately believed, hoping that it'd give me the sense of identity that I lacked. I figured that if I could make others like me, then I would be able to finally like myself. The ironic consequence is that the actions I took to like myself, such as heavy drinking, only served to further increase my dislike of myself.

Sobriety forced me to look at something I hadn't previously considered: Who the hell am I? There was the possibility that I wouldn't even like the person I actually was. If you're considering permanent sobriety or if you just hopped on the wagon, this is also likely to be one of your biggest concerns.

Of course, few people admit to worrying about an identity crisis. Instead, they mention their worries about socializing. This is a different expression of the same problem. You're worried that you won't know who you are, what you like, or if you'll even like the person you really are.

Since that seems like a heavy dose of psychoanalysis, I'll state the problem differently: if you have a strong identity which is independent of alcohol, why would you wonder what to do or how you'll feel once you stop drinking? You would already know your likes, dislikes, and exactly how to live your life without alcohol.

If I decided that you could no longer have candy, we'd very quickly find out how much of your identity is tied to candy. Most people wouldn't give it much thought, because while candy is delicious, it's not a big deal in their lives. The remaining people would either experience nothing—because they never eat candy—or they would panic—because of how they relate to it. The latter group clearly has an unhealthy relationship.

Anytime that you're worried about how to live without something, it is a significant part of your identity. If you're wondering how you'll live without booze, you have an unhealthy relationship with it. You're unsure of how you'll socialize, or even what you'll do in general because a large part of your identity is now facing (or currently undergoing) extinction.

Believe it or not, that's fine and it's part of the process. One thing I wish I'd understood about sobriety is how little I understood myself. Secondly, I wish that once I understood myself, I paid more attention to myself. The signals about what you like are always there, but you won't listen to this signal while your battle for external approval persists.

I'm not going to tell you how to socialize without alcohol or how to substitute drinking with other activities. I'm also not going to tell you exactly what type of life to build. Instead, I will tell you how to find and amplify the voice that's been telling you what you like all along.

As the old saying goes: *"Give a man a fish and he'll eat for a day. Teach a man to fish, and he'll eat for the rest of his life."*

I am teaching you how to fish. I'm giving you the strategy for finding yourself even when you're unsure of who you are. Someone out there is worried about achieving sobriety because they literally can't imagine life without booze. If that's you, or you're struggling to cope with sobriety because you don't know what to do with yourself, the following section will be illuminating.

How to Connect With The Real You

I simply have life experience, albeit learned the hard way, and I'm not an idiot about spotting patterns. My only goal is to point out that my knowledge of self comes from real life experiences and not textbook theories. Furthermore, finding yourself is ONLY developed from real experience or its first cousins: anecdotes and personal observation.

I gave an official disclaimer at the beginning of this book, but here it is again:

I'm not a medical professional. My advice should not be taken in the place of a medical professional. I'm just a guy who did certain things which worked. When I suggested the same things (or slight variations) to other people, they also worked. I hope the same happens with you.

Now just sit there. Seriously. Do nothing, except remain sober. Well, not exactly nothing. You can play video games, take walks, or see your friends if that's what you would do while drinking. Within reason, enjoy all the activities which you would have enjoyed under the influence of alcohol, except enjoy them while you're sober. At some point, you're going to feel uncomfortable. That's alright and to be expected.

That's right; I'm intentionally suggesting that you experience a bit of discomfort, but not so much that you break down and decide to start drinking again. You want to feel what your life is like without drinking. If you're like 99.9% of people, you'll find that a lot of activities simply don't feel the same. It doesn't mean there's something wrong with you. Remember, the whole point of this section (and this book) is to help you.

If you're part of the 0.1% who experiences nothing, and life goes on as usual, congratulations! You're such an outlier that I can't imagine why you picked up this book in the first place. Thank you for your support. However, I seriously doubt that you're in such a small sliver of space because that's simply the nature of probability.

After I stopped drinking, I tried to go out to karaoke a few times; I was convinced that I loved karaoke. However, I don't go much anymore because I noticed certain things about my once-favorite pastime. If I go to a karaoke bar which starts at 10 PM and closes at 2 a.m., I might sing 4 to 5 songs. Logistically, if each song is 5 minutes (and that's a big IF), that leaves me with over 3.5 hours to be in a bar with nothing to do.

When I drank, I could force myself to stay out until closing time. I did this by convincing myself that I was waiting for a chance to sing. After alcohol became a non-option, I was forced to accept that I didn't like karaoke that much. Yes, I enjoyed singing, but the entire event of *"going out to karaoke"* was just an excuse to drink. Of course, I didn't come to this realization immediately after I got sober.

It took a few karaoke sessions of being bored out of my mind and experiencing mild degrees of angst. Each of these experiences was important because they provided me with perspective. I still maintain that for some drinkers, heavy alcoholism is a result of lacking self-knowledge.

Sometimes, to learn something new, you must forget what you already know. At the very least, you must be willing to regard what you THINK you know with enough skepticism to entertain the possibility of your current beliefs being false.

The reality is that you don't NEED to drink. Despite the depth or intensity of your addiction, you were not born this way. Unless you had an exceptionally unfortunate childhood, you did not grow up this way either. This means that, at one point or another, alcoholism was assimilated into your personality, hobbies, and preferences. Therefore, your first course of action must be to experience your activities, hobbies, and preferences WITHOUT being under the influence.

Take note of the feeling; it may not be immediate, but you will encounter a moment familiar to all recovering alcoholics. You experience a moment where drinking is something which you do out of habit, but your attempt at sobriety interrupts your normal response of grabbing a drink.

You will know this moment because you'll have the unmistakable feeling of *"What the fuck am I doing here? I hate this shit."* Before you start to hate yourself for experiencing this feeling, excuse yourself from the situation and commence the next step. Finally, do NOT forget that feeling of angst.

Now comes introspection. Sadness and frustration are useless if you don't learn from their cause and do what you can to prevent the experiences from happening again in the future. While the specifics of your frustration and angst will vary based upon your interests and personality, the general theme will be the same.

Either:

You won't feel like something is enjoyable without alcohol

OR...

You won't feel like yourself when you're doing something familiar.

The first problem is easier to deal with. In an ideal world, you'd only experience the first problem when you cease drinking. This is because if you only enjoy certain activities while under the influence, you likely don't enjoy them in general. My personal examples were waiting in the bar between karaoke sessions or meeting large groups of people at once. At the end of the day, they were just excuses to drink.

Thankfully, the solution to these problems is incredibly straightforward: simply don't partake in the activity anymore. As much as I love karaoke, I really hate what I've got to do to partake in it. As of the date of this publication, I haven't been out to karaoke in over 2 years. Being part of a large group and hanging out in a bar are two things I simply don't enjoy. Therefore, I stopped doing them. The problem becomes a little more interesting when you look at things through the lens of the second problem.

I went through a phase where I loved football. However, after my sobriety, I thought football fell into the category of things which no longer interested me, but now I'm once again interested. Football did not become more interesting; if anything, the politicization of the sport has ruined football for me. Ultimately, I had to learn to enjoy the sport independently of craving booze.

The problems of the second type, where you don't feel like yourself doing something familiar, are more subtle and require a different approach. When you don't feel like yourself, but still partake in certain activities, this tells us one thing: whether by compulsion or obligation, you continue to do something despite it being uncoupled from alcohol. This is the most telling sign of a truly unhealthy relationship with alcohol.

I say this because the typical response is for people to withdraw themselves from activities they engaged in while under the influence. The only reasons people choose not to do so is either because they can't (professional obligation) or won't (social addiction). You feel out of place and *"not like yourself"* because you are now forced to engage life on a very different set of terms than the ones you are used to.

For many of us, drinking is also a coping mechanism. I used to drink before dates. At my last job as a customer service representative, I used to regularly get drunk before heading into work. I also started drinking before family gatherings and mundane social situations. These were the situations in which I felt I needed alcohol.

This period of introspection, of experiencing the pain and discomfort points, is meant to reveal the parts of yourself which have been masked by alcoholism. Excessive drinking is the result of trying to escape weaknesses and bolster inadequacies. Whether out of boredom, anxiety, frustration, or self-loathing, we drink to avoid these feelings.

The irony of a mind-altering substance is that it is often the only way we know how to feel normal.

After identifying your pain points, engage in activities which either allow you to slyly avoid or directly confront your pain points. While I personally recommend confronting weaknesses, this is a function of my personality rather than a necessity. If a person's natural disposition is introversion, suggesting their involvement in political grassroots movements and fundraising would be silly. Likewise, if they're naturally extroverted, suggesting long solitary hikes through the local park would be equally as foolish.

At the end of the day, wherever you look is where you're going to find yourself. A big indication of your real personality are the activities that naturally appeal to you. I've always believed that I was extroverted, as I drank to become the life of the party. Upon reaching sobriety, I realized that I craved connection and recognition; while I still leaned on the extroverted side, I am much closer to an introvert than I previously believed. I only took on certain extroverted qualities because I believed they would help me attain the things I desired.

This is how you will find yourself again. The mistake that many people make is to quit drinking without knowledge of themselves. Given the role that alcohol plays in their lives, this is the psychological equivalent of jumping off of a cruise ship at night in the middle of the ocean. You won't have anything to grasp, nor will you know which way the direction of safety is. It won't be long before you drown, except, in this case, drowning means returning to alcohol because you don't know any better.

Acknowledgements

This is the second major book that I've self-published. While I had some help when I published *"Not Caring What Other People Think Is A Superpower"*, it was nothing compared to the magnitude of assistance I received this time around. I want to acknowledge the people who made this book possible.

Jon "The Architect" Persson

Jon has been my designer and advisor for over 2 years. A talented good advisor is already a tremendous asset, but in the creation of this book he also displayed his impressive graphic design skills. Not only did Jon create the book cover, he also did the typesetting and design work of the book's interior.

I wrote a great book, but Jon's technical and artistic talents transformed it into an eye-catching, memorable, stand-out masterpiece.

"The Real" Dylan Madden

I've been corresponding with Dylan for a while. He reached out to me to write the foreword for his book *"Think And Go Hustle"* and from there, I began to pay more attention to the message he was promoting. His authenticity and character not only proved to me that he's a guy who's going places, but also that he's someone I could trust.

When I realized that I needed help bringing this book to life and coordinating it's many moving parts, I immediately reached out to Dylan. He's helped spread the awareness of the book as well as manage the connection between me and all the people working on it.

I'm just the writer. All roads to the promotion of the book go through Dylan Madden. I'm sure that you'll be hearing more of his name in the future.

Dennis "The Professional" Demori

Dennis is a professional copywriter of the highest caliber. I wanted the best to write the copy for the landing sales page *soberletters.com*, so having Dylan approach him with the offer was an easy decision. Dennis normally charges a king's ransom for his talents, but he believed in me and the message of this book so much that he gave me a solid discount. However, this does not mean he discounted the quality of his work.

I was genuinely surprised by the time he took to find out how I viewed my book as a solution for people who are struggling with alcoholism. As a result of Dennis' attention to detail, I have an excellent sales page that is helping others find this book and be transformed by the words inside.

Gabrielle Seunagal, Yusef Wateef, Michelle Rupert

These three have no idea how much they're responsible for bringing this book to life. Their editing and proofreading skills breathed new life into my prose. Between the three of them, they caught basic typos, offered suggestions on how to better present my ideas, and made this book way better than it would have been otherwise.

For my books in the future, I will definitely be relying on their skills and input to help me produce a top-notch product.

Sean McHugh

Sean took an interest in the book from the moment I announced it and offered to finance some of the production costs. The internet may have removed the gatekeepers required to publish a book, but they didn't make it free.

All of the people on this list required compensation for lending their talents. The funding that Sean contributed greatly lessened the financial burden of producing this book. As a result, I was able to afford all the necessary help to make this book a reality.

Made in the USA
San Bernardino, CA
15 August 2019